Vinicius Junior: The Inspiring Story of One of Soccer's Star Forwards

An Unauthorized Biography

By: Clayton Geoffreys

Copyright © 2024 by Calvintir Books, LLC

All rights reserved. Neither this book nor any portion thereof may be reproduced or used in any manner whatsoever without the express written permission. Published in the United States of America.

Disclaimer: The following book is for entertainment and informational purposes only. The information presented is without contract or any type of guarantee assurance. While every caution has been taken to provide accurate and current information, it is solely the reader's responsibility to check all information contained in this article before relying upon it. Neither the author nor publisher can be held accountable for any errors or omissions. Under no circumstances will any legal responsibility or blame be held against the author or publisher for any reparation, damages, or monetary loss due to the information presented, either directly or indirectly. This book is not intended as legal or medical advice. If any such specialized advice is needed, seek a qualified individual for help.

Trademarks are used without permission. Use of the trademark is not authorized by, associated with, or sponsored by the trademark owners. All trademarks and brands used within this book are used with no intent to infringe on the trademark owners and only used for clarifying purposes.

This book is not sponsored by or affiliated with the Série A, Segunda División B, La Liga, Copa do Brasil, Copa del Rey, Copa Sudamericana, Primeira Liga, Copa Libertadores, Campeonato Carioca, UEFA Champions League, FIFA Club World Cup, Supercopa de España & UEFA Super Cup, its teams, the players, or anyone involved with them.

Visit my website at www.claytongeoffreys.com
Cover photo by All-Pro Reels is licensed under CC BY-SA 2.0 / modified from original

Table of Contents

Foreword..1

Introduction 3

Chapter 1: Childhood & Early Life 10

    Escola Flamengo and Futsal Beginnings..........................12

    Flamengo Academy 14

Chapter 2: Professional Career 20

    Brazilian Professional Soccer...26

    Emotional Farewell to Flamengo 31

    Introduction at Real Madrid 33

    Real Madrid Castilla...36

    Real Madrid 2018-2019 41

    Real Madrid 2019-2020 45

    Covid-19 Shutdown..48

    Real Madrid 2020-2021 52

    Real Madrid 2021-2022 58

    Real Madrid 2022-2023 66

Turning Points 70

Vinicius Encounters Racist Abuse 74

Chapter 3: International Career 78

Brazil U-15, U-17, and U-20 79

Brazil First Team 81

2022 FIFA World Cup 85

Chapter 4: Personal Life 94

Philanthropic Work 97

Chapter 5: Future and Legacy 101

Final Word/About the Author 110

References 116

Foreword

Vinicius Junior, also known as Vini Jr., played at Flamengo in Brazil before joining Real Madrid in 2018, where he quickly became one of soccer's most exciting young players. He has been vital to Real Madrid's success, helping the team secure three La Liga titles and two UEFA Champions League victories as of this writing. He is also recognized as the youngest player to score in two Champions League finals, even surpassing Messi.

Vinicius Jr. has represented Brazil in international competitions, including the 2021 Copa America and the 2022 World Cup qualifiers, contributing to the national team's success. His remarkable skills and potential make him one of the best young players in soccer today. Thank you for purchasing *Vinicius Junior: The Inspiring Story of One of Soccer's Star Forwards*. In this unauthorized biography, we will learn Vinicius Junior's incredible life story and impact on the game of soccer. Hope you enjoy and if you do, please do not forget to leave a review!

Also, check out my website to join my exclusive list where I let you know about my latest books. To thank you for your purchase, I'll gift you free copies of some of my other books at **claytongeoffreys.com/goodies**.

Or, if you don't like typing, scan the QR code here to go there directly.

Cheers,

Clayton Geoffreys

Visit me at www.claytongeoffreys.com

Introduction

It's a scene that any soccer fan can immediately recognize and appreciate. It was a lovely late spring Saturday afternoon, full of sunshine and warm temperatures, and the setting was a proud old stadium in a mid-sized city. Vendors milled about hawking snacks and cold drinks, while the excited sounds of proud supporter songs and chants filled the air in anticipation.

That scene is no doubt similar to many others taking place around the world, as organized groups of 11 young men or women battle it out on the pitch, chasing the glory of a hard-fought victory. On this day, it was the supporters of the beloved home team, the Spanish squad of Valencia FC. The restless crowd was packed in shoulder to shoulder, eager to see how their local side would match up with the behemoths of the Spanish La Liga, Real Madrid.

In many ways, this scene is the embodiment of what draws so many people to what has been called "The Beautiful Game." The passion, the energy, the suspense of a close match as the clock makes its inevitable crawl toward full time, the home supporters clinging to hope as they wait to explode in a victory celebration. These are all essential elements that make soccer the most popular game in the world. Then, like a needle scratching the surface of a record, everything changes. This is where this particular sunny story gives way to a darker turn.

Time was running out and Valencia clung desperately to the narrowest of leads, 1-0, with less than 15 minutes remaining on the clock. As the visitors were lining up to attempt a crucial free kick within scoring range, one of Real Madrid's transcendent young talents, Vinicius Jr.—known to some as Vini Jr. or just simply Vini—could be seen pointing and gesturing toward the fans situated in the stands behind the goal.

Attempting to get the attention of the referee, the young Brazilian phenom was shouting that the fans behind the goal were taunting him with racist insults and vile tropes, all directed at him because of the color of his skin. Vinicius was clearly livid, shouting to anyone within hearing distance, "He called me a monkey," and was pointing into the crowd at a specific spectator indicating, "It was him! It was him!"

His Real Madrid teammates as well as members of the Valencia squad tried to calm Vini down, but without success. Finally responding to his pleas, the referee called for a pause in the match, instituting the anti-racism protocol implemented by La Liga to respond to just this type of occurrence. During the pause, the public address announcer could be heard admonishing the crowd, warning that any additional racist chants would result in the match being suspended and the spectators ejected from the stadium.

Real Madrid goalkeeper Thibaut Courtois assured Vinicius that the team had his back, and they would all walk off the pitch in solidarity with their hurting teammate if he wanted them to. Vini also received a similar message of support from his veteran coach, Carlo Ancelotti, who told him that he was inclined to pull his players from the field in protest as well.

As empathetic and well-meaning as those messages were intended to be, leaving injustice and hatred unaddressed and shying away from a confrontation are not in Vinicius' DNA. He was determined not to allow his detractors to get the best of him.

Signaling his desire to remain in the game, Vinicius joined his teammates in walking back onto the pitch as the match resumed after the pause in action. Minutes later, a still-agitated Vinicius engaged in a scuffle with a Valencia player following an aggressive challenge. Valencia players then rushed to the defense of their own, one of whom restrained Vini in a headlock in the process.

As Vinicius began to fight back, attempting to disentangle himself from the headlock, the referee came over to the scrum, once again pausing the match to sort out the problem. For his part in the melee, Vinicius was shown a red card, earning him an expulsion from the contest—and, of course, howls of derisive clapping and laughter from the fans.

Following the contest, a clearly disgruntled Vinicius had strong words for what had just occurred in the old stadium. "The prize that the racists won was my sending-off!" Vinicius declared on Instagram, making it clear whom he thought bore the brunt of the responsibility for allowing the situation to get to that point. Vini then cleverly re-purposed the catchphrase of the league, "It's not football. It's LaLiga," not-so-subtly implying that the Spanish league's lack of serious action to combat the growing problem of racism in sports was glaring and deplorable.

Fast forward to almost a year later, March 2024. Same pitch, same fans, and many of the same players were present, all aware of the circumstances that had marred the previous year's encounter. Meanwhile, Valencia's supporters, most of whom were not involved in the vile and discriminatory behavior exhibited last year, felt unfairly maligned; they had been painted with a broad brush as racist due to the unruly actions of a minority and they were there to make their voices heard.

Tensions were running high in the stands, and a ubiquitous police presence was in place to respond to any trouble that might arise. Just like the contest the year before, the home team got off to a good start, with two scores on the board as the first 45 minutes gave way to a handful of minutes of stoppage time. As the waning minutes of the half were ticking down, Vinicius deftly gathered a cross in the box that had deflected off a defender and tapped it into the net to slice the lead in half.

Grabbing the ball from the goal and running back to midfield, he was then showered by boos and insults. Vini stopped and gazed back in the direction of the stands that had been ground zero for the previous year's ugly incident. This time, however, there was no agitation on his face, no sign of being upset by the boorish behavior on display.

Vinicius, who had spent much of the intervening time leading the effort to point out the problems of racism in La Liga and engaged in discussions about the best ways for the league to respond, appeared composed and resolute. Perhaps borrowing a gesture from the black power protests of the 1968 United States Olympians on the podium in Mexico, Vinicius lifted a closed fist, signifying strength in the face of oppression.

This, of course, brought more boos from the crowd, but it did not seem to faze Vini in the slightest. His show of strength had carried the day and, perhaps best of all, denied the opposition's raucous fans the pleasure of seeing him lose control again.

Growing up as a child in Brazil, Vinicius, like so many young boys and girls throughout the country, had dreams of achieving glory on the soccer pitch. He likely imagined scoring goals for his country and accruing the adoration that comes with being a famous and successful athlete. Being a celebrity athlete who was thrust into the struggle to eradicate the scourge of racism in sports was surely one of the last things that he could have imagined for his future self. Yet here he was, a pillar of tranquility and resolve, standing tall and resolute in a storm of insults and derision.

Although it was a simple gesture, it was also a powerful statement from a young person who has not shied away from the mantle of being an agent of change. Even though he did not ask for the role, Vinicius has now become one of the most important figures in history to address the problem of racism in sports.

"I have a purpose in life," Vinicius offered via Twitter, "and if I have to keep suffering so that future generations won't have to go through these types of situations, I'm ready and prepared."

So, how does a promising young football talent from the impoverished outskirts of Rio de Janeiro grow into a prodigious internationally renowned soccer superstar, ultimately being tapped as a UNESCO Goodwill Ambassador for his work to improve education and combat racism and discrimination?

This is the story of Vinicius Jr., and fortunately for all of us, his story is just getting started.

Chapter 1: Childhood & Early Life

The sensational Brazilian soccer star that the world has come to know as Vinicius Jr. is one of the most talented, well-paid, and outspoken athletes alive today. While the exact figure is undisclosed, estimates of his current contract with the La Liga powerhouse Real Madrid are in the range of $10,000,000 per year.[i]

In addition to his robust salary, Vini Jr. has signed many lucrative endorsement deals with numerous international companies such as Nike, Dolce & Gabbana, and Pepsi, just to name a few, which adds to his already impressive yearly income. One estimate of his net worth in 2024 places his overall financial value at $20,000,000.[ii]

These figures have allowed the young soccer star to enjoy a life of privilege, even sometimes traveling the globe in the company of movie stars and professional athletes from the NBA and NFL. Although he can now frequently be seen courtside at an NBA game, trading jerseys with LeBron James or dapping up Shai Gilgeous-Alexander, Vini Jr. has not always known such fame and fortune.

Vinicius Jose Paixao de Oliveira Jr. was born on July 12, 2000, in Sao Goncalo, a working-class neighborhood of Rio de

Janeiro, Brazil. Raised by his parents Tatiana Fernanda Vinicius, who is of Congolese descent, and Brazilian Jose Paixao de Oliveira, young Vini grew up with his two younger brothers and one older sister in a very modest home. His father Jose was in the construction business and was the sole wage earner in the household. Vini's mother Fernanda spent her days as a homemaker, looking after little Vini and his siblings.

Although the family was not prosperous, Vini nevertheless had a happy childhood. Known for his frequent smiling and infectious laugh even as a young boy, Vini found it easy to make friends in his neighborhood. He has stated of his childhood that he was always on the street, playing soccer or other games with his neighborhood friends.

Vini once famously stated that, as a child, the only reasons that he would return home was to play the FIFA video game or to eat or sleep! Ironically, it has been reported that young Vini's favorite team to use in that FIFA video game was FC Barcelona, where he could execute shrewd moves on the virtual pitch using an avatar of one of his most beloved childhood soccer idols, the great Lionel Messi.[iii]

Escola Flamengo and Futsal Beginnings

Vini's first formal experience with organized soccer came at the age of six, when he attended a soccer training school affiliated with one of Rio's more famous teams, Flamengo. The Escola Flamengo, owned and run by Carlos Abrantes, was not exactly known for its affluence, as their tattered goal nets and an imperfect pitch with patchy grass suggest.[iv] From early on, however, there were signs that young Vini was a special talent.

Abrantes, who also served as the school's soccer coach, later reflected, "Vinicius immediately stood out for his dribbling ability and speed. When we played in tournaments, teams tried to man-mark him, but they never managed to keep him quiet. He was too quick, too direct. No one could keep up with him. He was unstoppable."[v]

At the Escola Flamengo, Vini began to participate in organized Futsal, a typically smaller, indoor version of soccer, played 5-on-5 on a hard surface, such as a basketball court. In fact, Vini now credits his time as a youngster on the Futsal court as integral to his technical skill on the pitch.

Describing his early foundation as a player, Vini reported that, in addition to playing soccer on the streets with his friends in the neighborhood as a child, "Futsal also helped me. Everyone says that Brazilian players have a lot of quality and I think it's because we play in small spaces, we started playing in the street when we were young and always with older people. All that helps us."[vi]

While young Vini was experiencing his first taste of organized football at school, his family situation at home was also undergoing some important changes. Vini's father took a job as a building manager in Sao Paulo, leaving his mother to attend to the children at home. Due to the family's precarious financial situation, Carlos Abrantes, who is frequently credited for discovering Vini, often helped the impoverished young boy acquire soccer gear such as second-hand cleats and a bag for him to transport his gear to and from his home every day.

Despite the financial struggles faced by the family, Vini's mother always ensured that her soccer-loving son made it to school every day as well as to all of the training sessions and matches. He always had her full support.

Vini continued to participate in the Flamengo soccer school, finding success and rapidly building his soccer skills. In 2009, at the age of nine, Vini participated in tryouts for the Futsal Academy at Flamengo. While his quickness and technical skill impressed those in charge of selecting team members, the coaches nevertheless asked Vini to participate in another year of training at the school prior to joining the academy because of his young age.

This fateful decision proved to be a significant early turning point in Vini's soccer career. With the guidance and approval of his family, Vini opted not to return to the Futsal Academy at Flamengo. In fact, he decided to eschew futsal altogether, choosing instead to pursue training for traditional soccer on an outdoor pitch.

Given his natural ability and drive to compete, it is likely that if Vini had decided to double down and pursue a career in professional futsal, he would have been wildly successful. He might have even come to be known as the greatest futsal player of all time if he had taken that course of action. But little did he know at the time, making that early choice to concentrate on soccer undoubtedly changed his future. His life would take a far different and much more lucrative course than it would have been if he had limited his soccer stylings to the indoor pitch of futsal. So, futsal's loss was most definitely football's gain!

Flamengo Academy

In 2010 at the age of 10, Vinicius tried out and earned a spot in the soccer academy at Flamengo. Somewhat curiously, despite

Vinicius' skill at offense and prolific goal-scoring ability, young Vini wrote that his favored position was as a defensive-minded left-back on his intake paperwork for the academy. Some have speculated that this was due to the fact that his favorite player and role model on the Flamengo first team played left back. Nevertheless, despite this designation, Vini's future would lie in an attacking position. And it would not take long before this began to be noticed by the higher-ups at the academy.

The director of the Flamengo youth system, Carlos Noval, remembered Vini finding quick success in his new environs. "He was head and shoulders above the rest," Noval told one reporter. "Right from the start, he used to go at defenders, exactly as he does today. He wasn't scared of anything. The way he could dribble at pace was impressive. He could change direction in a flash."

Additionally, Noval noted that not only did Vini have tremendous success on the pitch from the star but he also seemed to be having a lot of fun. "If I had to pick one word to describe him," he continued, "It would be *joyous*. Wherever he went, he won people over with his smile and attitude. It was contagious."[v]

Noval also noted that, in addition to the joy that Vini so obviously experienced on the pitch, there was also an edge, an inner drive to excel, that perhaps was due to the many hardships that had beset his family. "He gave everything on the pitch, knowing that football would allow him to help his family and those around him. That was in his mind even from a young age."[iv]

Indeed, while Vini was busy impressing his new teammates and coaches at the Flamengo Academy, his family continued to make countless sacrifices in order to fuel his chance at football glory. Some months, money was so hard to come by that the family did not have the cash to pay the school fees required to keep him in training. From time to time, this meant that Noval would allow the family to skip a payment or two just to ensure that Vini could remain with the team. They would even sometimes provide Vini with food when he did not have enough to eat.[vii]

To make matters even more difficult, Vini Sr. was now busy working 200 miles away in Sao Paulo, so the task of ensuring the young rising football star was able to make the 90-minute trek to the academy training ground fell to his mother Fernanda. And worse still, she did not drive. Thus, Vini's mother would escort him approximately two-thirds of the way on the slow, antiquated public bus system with his baby brother Jose in tow, and Vini would make the last leg of the trip on a different bus. Then, Fernanda and baby Jose would wait for him to return following practice, sometimes as long as three or four hours, when they would all load up on the original bus for the return trip home.

Eventually, the family was able to secure private van transportation to make the trip shorter and easier for Vini, however this, too, was a short-term solution.[iv] Finally, when he was 12 years old, the family made the difficult decision for young Vinicius to move in with his uncle Ulysses, who lived just a short drive from the Flamengo Academy's training center. If the move out of his family home was challenging, young Vinicius never let on. By all accounts, he was well taken care of in his new situation.

By age 14, it was becoming apparent that Vinicius Jr. was a rare talent. He was beginning to be viewed as one of the best young players in Rio and, as such, his family agreed to allow his burgeoning career to be unofficially guided by TFM, a renowned Brazilian sports management company. Because Brazilian law did not permit a young player to sign and execute an official contract to be represented by an agent, the firm was taking a gamble on Vini's future by investing heavily in his career with nothing but a "gentleman's agreement" in place that once he reached maturity he would then sign on the dotted line for TFM in the form of an official contract of representation.[vii]

That investment in Vini's future by TFM not only came in the form of him now having access to top-of-the-line gear and instruction but it also carried very real benefits for his economically struggling family. The financial support provided by TFM allowed Vini's father to return to Rio to better support his son as he moved up the ranks of promising young Brazilian soccer players.

Additionally, the family was able to rent an apartment close to the Flamengo training center, which allowed them to once more become a daily part of the budding superstar's day-to-day life. TFM even funded young Vini's travel and participation in two training opportunities in the United States at facilities used by professional American sporting clubs.

With this terrific infusion of resources now available to him, Vini's performance on the pitch soon grew to new heights. In addition to his participation in the Flamengo youth squads, Vini also began to have opportunities to suit up for his country and represent Brazil in international youth competitions.

Playing for Brazil in the South American U-15 Championship, the 14-year-old Vinicius netted six goals along the way to helping the squad take the first-place trophy. By 2017, Vini was named the top player in the South American U-17 Championship, and his future was looking extraordinarily bright.

Given his rapid ascent through the youth leagues, it was seen as only a matter of time before the call to join the Flamengo first team would occur. But as fate would have it, it was not just Flamengo who had their eyes on the young soccer phenom. A bidding war was beginning to develop among the world's top-flight clubs over who would have the rights to negotiate with Flamengo for the chance to sign him.

For Vini Jr., the world was about to change in ways that might have been impossible to imagine a few short years prior.

Chapter 2: Professional Career

In May 2017, with the beginning of the 2017-2018 campaign only days away, Vini Jr. got the call that he had been waiting for. Fresh off scoring two goals and assisting with two others in a U-17 match for Flamengo, Vini was asked to join the Flamengo first team squad as they prepared for their opening match of the Brazilian Serie A season.

While Flamengo head coach Ze Roberto had high hopes for his young star, he also knew that it was important to temper expectations for the 16-year-old, who had not yet had even a minute of professional soccer under his belt.

"It would be utopian to say that a 16-year-old is ready, but he has done very well in the younger categories of the club," stated the coach in the run-up to Vini joining the first team squad in training. "On the basis of his merits, he will start to play. He is a young man with a lot of talent, and it was time to put all this potential at the service of the professionals."[viii]

Given his rapid and celebrated rise through the Flamengo system, it is no surprise that news of the young Vini's successes reverberated across the larger ecosystem of world soccer. In addition to catching the attention of the Flamengo first team coaching staff, scouts from the highest levels of international soccer were also making their way to Brazil to get a look at the young budding superstar to judge him with their own eyes.

It was clear right away that the international talent hunters liked what they were seeing in Vinicius Jr. Rumors started to circulate in Rio as well as in the media that the biggest soccer clubs in the world were involved in bidding for his services. In the spring of 2017, even before Vini could suit up for his initial foray with the first team at Flamengo, Spanish newspapers began to circulate stories of the two giants of the La Liga—Barcelona and Real Madrid—each preparing transfer bids for the 16-year-old. Thus, it was against this fervent backdrop of hype and anticipation that the professional career of Vinicius Jr. would begin.

Decked out in the No. 20 jersey, Vini saw his first professional minutes for Flamengo's first team on May 13, 2017, when he came on as a substitute in the 82nd minute in a 1-1 contest against Clube Atletico Mineiro. Despite coming up empty in his search for the late game-winning goal, Vini was nevertheless excited to finally get to run with the first team. In an uneven initial performance, Vini admitted after the contest that he felt some nervousness upon entering the contest.

"The fans were chanting my name, and I got nervous," he remarked after the game, before adding, "I want to thank my coach for giving me this opportunity, and I hope it's a year of many wins." [ix]

Perhaps just as big to Vini as logging his first big-time professional minutes, Vini had the honor of meeting and trading jerseys after the game with another of his childhood soccer idols, Robinho. Referencing the post-game jersey swap, Vini noted, "Robinho's been my idol since I was a little kid and today, I was able to play against him. That's why I asked him for his shirt."[ix]

Given the domestic and international interest in the young rising star, Flamengo took the opportunity to ink Vini Jr. to a lucrative contract extension through 2019, raising his transfer release clause fee from 30 to 45 million Euros. This was a staggering sum for a 16-year-old player with less than 10 minutes of first-team football under his belt!

Indeed, a high-dollar release fee for an unproven young international talent might be a deterrent to many clubs on the lookout for future stars. After all, who knows how a young player may develop, even a player with immense natural gifts such as Vini? Plus, add in the uncertainty of him moving to another country, possibly another continent, with the inherent language barriers and cultural differences, and it could begin to make less daring soccer clubs rethink taking such a massive financial gamble on an untested teenage prodigy. Then again, the giants of Spain's La Liga—Real Madrid and their bitter rivals, Barcelona—have never been accused of being shrinking violets when it comes to handing out large contracts to soccer prospects. A bidding war was beginning to take shape.

According to reports, it was Barcelona who made the first move. Barca, who had been scouting young Vini for three years by that point, initially felt confident they would be the club that would land the coveted young player. According to some accounts, there was already a "handshake agreement" in place between Barca and those representing Vini Jr.[x] Meanwhile, Barca's rivals Real Madrid were relative latecomers in the Vini sweepstakes by comparison, having only been on the scent of the youngster for about 70 days. But despite this discrepancy in time and money spent in scouting Vinicius, the race between the La Liga rivals was seen as a close one. When all was said and done, it was Barcelona who came through with the greater amount of cash to offer the young phenom for his services.

Real Madrid, however, were not to be outdone by simple numbers on a ledger sheet. Even though they were offering a contract of lesser overall financial value, Los Blancos, as they are affectionately known to their followers, had another ace up their sleeve which they hoped would make their club a more appealing destination.

Under the leadership of savvy club president Florentino Perez, the club had adopted the "Galacticos" approach, meaning that they made a point of signing the best and brightest soccer stars from around the world while they were still young. This approach had allowed Real Madrid to collect some of the biggest names in international soccer, including former players such as David Beckham, Zinedine Zidane, Luis Figo, and Vini's fellow Brazilians Ronaldo (de Lima) and Robinho. So, when Vini's representatives met with officials from Real Madrid, their handsome financial offer was bolstered by their commitment to surround Vinicius with enough talent to compete for Europe's greatest trophies for years to come.

In the end, the opportunity to compete for championships while playing alongside the greatest players in the world for the most decorated club in soccer history was just too tantalizing for Vini Jr. to pass up. On May 23, 2017, Real Madrid announced that they had signed the first teenage Galactico to a deal in the neighborhood of 46 million Euros (approximately $50 million U.S.).

The contract was one of the most lucrative professional soccer deals ever for a Brazilian, second only to Neymar Jr. It also set a financial record for a contract signed by a teenaged soccer player at the time. Although the financial and tactical reasons that contributed to the signing have gotten the lion's share of attention, it was not a decision completely dictated by those factors, however. Vini Jr.'s heart also played a key role in the decision. When asked about why he landed on Real Madrid as his destination, Vini Jr. simply expressed the obvious.

"I want to play for the biggest team in the world, Hala Madrid!"[xi]

Despite signing on the dotted line with Madrid, Vinicius' arrival on the pitch for Los Blancos was anything but instantaneous. The governing body for international soccer, FIFA, in an effort to protect underage players, sets conditions on how and when clubs can secure international transfers for minors. With a few notable exceptions, FIFA has declared that players under the age of 18 are not allowed to transfer internationally.[xii] Thus Vini's new contract with Real Madrid required a loan clause that allowed Vini to remain in Brazil and continue to train and compete with Flamengo until he reached the age of 18.

Brazilian Professional Soccer

With the contract signed and all the drama in the rear-view mirror, Vini could now concentrate solely on doing what he loved most, playing soccer.

The next four games of his Flamengo first-team career began the same way as his first game, a second-half substitution in a closely contested game. On June 11, 2017, Vinicius was penciled in as a starter for Flamengo for the first time. Despite not tallying any goals or assists, the first start of his career indicated a growing confidence in his rapid development as a professional.

This increased confidence of the coaching staff in their young player was rewarded on August 10, 2017, in a second-round Copa Sudamericana match versus Chilean side Club Deportivo Palestino. Coming on as a substitute in the 72nd minute, the now 17-year-old Vini notched his first professional goal when a cross that he sent across the box caromed back to him, allowing him to put a solid strike on a ball that found the back of the net.

On the heels of his first professional goal, a mere nine days later, Vinicius netted his first scores in the Brazilian domestic Serie A competition with a second-half brace against Atletico Goianiense, scoring both goals in a 2-0 decision. Despite this performance, Vini continued to struggle to crack the starting lineup for Flamengo for much of the rest of the 2017 campaign.

Vini's final goal of the 2017 Serie A competition came in a match against Cruzeiro on November 8, 2017. In a stoppage-time thriller, Vini connected on a strike that found the back of the net, providing a two-goal cushion in the home team's winning performance.

As the season reached its conclusion, Vini Jr.'s final statistics for his initial year on the first team squad saw him make 36 appearances, including 4 starts, with 4 goals and 1 assist across all competitions. As for the club as a whole, Flamengo's 2017 campaign was largely mediocre, despite the advent of its young fledgling star. Flamengo notched a disappointing 6th-place finish in the Serie A standings, although they did have respectable showings as runners-up in both the Copa do Brasil and the Copa Sudamericana competitions.

Nevertheless, as the calendar turned to 2018, there was a lot of optimism in the air among the Flamengo supporters. Not only was their young striker ready to compete in his second season with the club but they were also welcoming back Paulo Carpegiani, a popular former player and manager, for his third stint as head coach. And with Vinicius' plans after turning 18 in July 2018—potentially meaning that the young phenom might not finish the season in Brazil—Flamengo supporters were eager to get off to a good start to the new campaign.

Like many professional soccer clubs around the world, Brazilian clubs have multiple opportunities to win trophies over the course of a year. These include the Campeonato Carioca (sponsored by the state football league of Rio de Janeiro), the Serie A (the top level of club football in Brazil), the Copa do Brasil (open to all professional clubs in Brazil), Copa Libertadores (South America's premier club soccer tournament), and Copa Sudamericana (South America's second-most prestigious club tournament).

The 2018 season began in January with the Campeonato Carioca competition, which is contested annually by the teams in the state league in Rio de Janeiro. As one of the "big four" clubs in the event, Flamengo typically had a leg up on the competition entering play. Placed in group A for the initial group stage of the competition, Flamengo wasted no time in compiling four wins against one draw, with young Vinicius supplying three goals, including the only tally in a 1-0 victory over Cabofriense. Despite their strong start, Flamengo had to settle for a third-place finish in the competition.

In the 2018 edition of the Copa Libertadores, Flamengo finished in second place in Group D, with two victories to go with four draws and zero defeats, qualifying them to move on to the Round of 16. In the group stage, young Vinicius continued to impress, netting another two-goal brace in a thrilling come-from-behind 2-1 win against the home-standing Ecuadorian side Emelec. Flamengo would eventually run into trouble in the Round of 16 against fellow Brazilian side Cruzeiro and were eliminated by the aggregate score of 2-1.

The Serie A season began in April 2018, with Flamengo on the road facing the hometown EC Vitoria squad. Flamengo fans were certainly overjoyed when within the first minute of the first Serie A match, Vinicius Jr. sent a pass ahead to the left foot of teammate Lucas Paqueta, who placed the ball into the bottom left corner for an immediate 1-0 lead to begin the game. That back-and-forth affair ended in a 2-2 draw, but Flamengo fans could be excused if they allowed themselves to dream about how special the team would be if young Vinicius could be convinced to stick around and see the season through to its conclusion.

Despite the uncertainty regarding his future plans, specifically when, exactly, he would make the move to Madrid following his 18th birthday in July, Vini appeared unphased by the worries or speculation about his future. He was having fun with the Flamengo first team, and things were looking good for them to begin the season.

In the first 12 games of the season, prior to a break in play due to the 2018 World Cup, Flamengo posted an impressive record of eight wins against three draws and one loss. Meanwhile, the young prodigy looked very much in form to be able to compete against his sometimes much older and more experienced opponents.

In a tough contest on the road against Ceara in the Brazilian city of Fortaleza on April 29, 2018, Vini once again delivered for Flamengo, scoring a brace and playing the entirety of the game. After a first half that appeared to be leading to a scoreless draw at halftime, Vinicius finally broke through with the first goal of the game, striking the ball with his right foot from the right side of the box and past the keeper to set the score at 1-0. Coming out of the halftime break, Vini remained in top form as he once again scored, this time from close range, giving Flamengo a two-goal lead in what would eventually become a 3-0 victory for the visitors from Rio.

Emotional Farewell to Flamengo

After matchday 12 on June 13th, all top-flight clubs in Serie A took a month-long hiatus while the 2018 World Cup competition got underway. While there were no matches during the hiatus, it would be a mistake to assume that all was quiet and uneventful with the club. Vinicius Jr. would be turning 18 on July 12th, meaning that his move to Real Madrid could be facilitated at any time. As part of the contract negotiations, Real Madrid had agreed to evaluate Vinicius after his 18th birthday. The plan was to have him participate in pre-season training with the club with the option of Madrid returning Vini to Flamengo on loan to finish the 2018 season at home in Brazil.

Fortunately for the Flamengo supporters, they would not have to wait long for a conclusion to the Vini Jr. transfer saga. On June 25, 2018, word reached the press that Real Madrid had rejected Flamengo's request to retain Vini for the remainder of the Serie A season, instead deciding to bring Vini to Madrid as soon as allowed by FIFA.[xiii] A farewell press conference was scheduled for June 26th so that Vini could face the Brazilian press one more time before he departed for Madrid.

In an emotional farewell address, Vini Jr. expressed sincere gratitude for the club and their faithful supporters. Still a teenager at the time, the young man stated, "I am saying goodbye to the club that did everything for me to fulfill my dream of playing for Real Madrid." Vini also acknowledged that he wanted to follow in the footsteps of other great Brazilian soccer players, such as Ronaldo and Ronaldinho, both of whom took their skills to La Liga.

Vini further indicated that, while he knew that he would have to learn a lot in order to compete at the highest level of international soccer, he felt that he was up to the task. "I am prepared for new challenges, and this is the biggest challenge in my life," said the young striker. "I want to adapt quickly to be happy at Madrid."[xiv]

With the press conference completed, Vinicius Jr.'s career at Flamengo was officially ending. Although Vini only competed for a short time for the first team Flamengo squad, he was leaving as a hero to many across his native country. While supporters undoubtedly wished for their home-grown star to remain in Brazil and demonstrate his mastery of the game in his native country, there was certainly hope that Vini would duplicate his domestic success on the world stage with Real Madrid and remain a valuable part of the legacy of Brazilian soccer in the process.

All told, across 69 matches in all competitions in 2017 and 2018, Vinicius Jr. tallied 29 starts for the Flamengo first-team side, scoring 14 goals and dishing out 4 assists along the way.[xv] On July 14, 2018, two days after his 18th birthday, Vinicius Jr. boarded a plane for Madrid, where he would finally get the opportunity to demonstrate his skills on international soccer's biggest stage.

Introduction at Real Madrid

On July 20, 2018, a mere eight days after he reached the age of 18, Vini was introduced to the media and Los Blancos supporters at one of the most hallowed grounds of international soccer, the Santiago Bernabeu Stadium in Madrid.

It was a time of transition for Real Madrid. Given the off-season departure of star striker Cristiano Ronaldo, many in the media and numerous supporters were curious to get a first look at the teenager who many were comparing to another Brazilian soccer superstar, Neymar. However, it was another famous Brazilian soccer legend that landed the honor of introducing the newest member of Real Madrid, Ronaldo Nazario.

Offering words of support to his young countryman, Ronaldo looked at Vini and remarked, "This is the best place you could be. We will be here to take care of you."[xvi]

Vinicius, seemingly aware of the always giant expectations for this venerated club, gave the assembled masses at the stadium what they wanted to hear. When asked about his objectives in joining Real Madrid, Vini remarked, "My objective is to win more. I always want to be on top, and that is why I've chosen Real Madrid and I want to conquer more championships."

Asked about the pressure to perform at a high level at Madrid, Vini responded, "I come from Flamengo, a club with a lot of pressure. I've become accustomed to it, but my family gives me all the support possible. I don't think about failure."[xvi]

Fans of Real Madrid would not have to wait long to see their newest acquisition perform on the pitch, as the squad traveled to the United States to participate in preseason friendly competitions just one week later.

Vini and his Real Madrid teammates faced Manchester United, the beasts of England's Premier League, at the Hard Rock

Stadium in Miami, Florida, on July 31, 2018. While young Vini was held scoreless in the competition, that did not stop the internet from overflowing with praise for the newcomer's performance on the pitch. Reactions from social media platform Twitter (now X) included comparisons to Neymar and Ronaldo as well as video clips of Vini from the match accompanied by the popular fire emoji.[xvii]

Based on his debut performance, fans of Real Madrid could not help but daydream about Vini's future with the club, already mentally placing new trophies in the club's trophy case. The future was indeed looking bright for Los Blancos and their supporters.

Returning to Spain, the squad began to prepare for the upcoming contests for the 2018-2019 season. Top-flight professional soccer clubs in Spain participate in La Liga, one of the top leagues in world soccer, featuring some of the best international players and their devoted fanbases. In addition to La Liga contests, the top finishers in La Liga each year earn a place in the coveted UEFA Champions League, where Europe's top clubs face off to determine on=field superiority.

The Europa League, while less prestigious than the Champions League, is another competition that allows prominent European clubs who did not qualify for the Champions League to face off against each other. Winners of the Champions League face off against the winner of the Europa League each year in the UEFA Super Cup.

Additionally, professional teams of all levels across Spain also participate yearly in the Copa del Rey competition, commonly called the Spanish Cup, a knockout tournament in which Real Madrid has had significant success over the years.

Vinicius Jr.'s first opportunity to put on the first-team jersey for Los Blancos took place on August 15, 2018, in a UEFA Super Cup competition against La Liga rivals Atletico Madrid in Tallinn, Estonia. Vini watched from the bench as his Real Madrid squad suffered a 4-2 defeat at the hands of their city-sharing rivals from Madrid. Similarly, although dressed and available as a reserve, Vini did not enter the La Liga season's opening match, a 2-0 win over Getafe.

Real Madrid Castilla

Despite the youngster showing promise in first-team training, Madrid coach Julen Lopetegui and Real Madrid upper management were not content to see their young prodigy remain on the bench when he could be training and getting valuable game action on the pitch. As such, they decided that Vinicius would participate in second-team drills and contests for Real Madrid Castilla, the U-21 development squad.

Reporting to Castilla in time for the season-opener, Vini started the match and played 72 minutes for the squad on August 26, 2018, recording no goals or assists. Vinicius' initial foray into the scoring column for Castilla came during the second game, a "mini-derby" versus the second-team squad from across town, Atletico Madrid, on September 2, 2018.

Atletico Madrid started the action early, with a third-minute goal on a free kick to give the home-standing Atletico a 1-0 lead. Not to be outdone, Vini took a pass from teammate Cristo Gonzalez, giving the ball a touch to lure out the goalkeeper, then slicing the ball to the far post to level the game, scoring his first goal wearing the Madrid logo.

Playing with the confidence of a seasoned veteran, Vini began to call for the ball and make thrilling runs toward the goal, and his teammates were happy to oblige. His aggression paid off in the form of a second goal at the 27-minute mark in the first half, as he fired an off-balance shot from distance that went past the keeper, giving him a first-half brace while at the same time sending Los Blanco fans into ecstasy with dreams of future championships, no doubt. Although Castilla would give up the equalizer in the 58th minute and the match ended in a 2-2 draw, there were two primary takeaways from the match.

The first and most enduring takeaway was that Vinicius was going to be a special talent and that his energy, enthusiasm, and leadership potential were nearly unlimited. The second takeaway, which unfortunately foreshadowed events yet to come for Vinicius, was that the combination of Vinicius' otherworldly talent along with his penchant for on-field displays of exuberant emotion sometimes brought out the worst in opposing players and fans.

Throughout the match, Atletico players resorted to harsh and intimidating tactics to contain Vinicius and keep him from taking over the game. Atletico defenders frequently made straight-line runs directly at Vini, sometimes taking him down in the process. One particularly heinous instance of this behavior was a second-half takedown of Vinicius by none other than Atletico's captain, Tachi, who concluded the incident by biting Vini on the back of the head! This resulted in both players receiving yellow cards for the interaction as well as the subsequent reaction to it.

Journalist Sam Sharpe, in a prescient comment, surmised that this may be only the first of many times that opponents would play dirty in an effort to stop Vinicius' dominance. "Vinicius may have to get used to that kind of attention," reported Sharpe. "Although it may not come as shockingly as that, it will inevitably be a common tactic used in attempt to stop him."[xviii]

Vini followed that performance with more solid showings for Castilla, first scoring the final goal of a 3-0 win over Salamanca's Unionistas CF and then drawing a key penalty that resulted in a goal and another win, this time over Cultural Leonesa by a final score of 2-1.

But Vini saved perhaps his most impressive performance for Castilla for his last match with the club. On October 21, 2018, Castilla faced home-standing Celta Vigo's B squad in a thrilling match that showcased the young Brazilian's skill and tenacity. Despite Vini's inspired first-half performance, the clubs went into the halftime break with Vigo having made the initial dent in the scoreboard, courtesy of a goal in the 39th minute.

In the second half, Vinicius Jr. practically put the team on his back, drawing foul after foul as the Vigo defenders struggled mightily to contain him. Vinicius could be seen visibly angry and muttering to himself, as he was the target of continued aggressive and sometimes even illegal defensive tactics. In the 83rd minute, Vini was brought down right outside of the box by a defender, giving him the opportunity to target the goal and win the hard-earned equalizer for Castilla. With a wall of three defenders between him and the goal, Vinicius uncorked a screaming strike that curled around the wall and quite amazingly continued to curve until it came to rest in the top left-hand corner of the goal. The flailing keeper had no chance to even come close to the ball as it settled into the net, setting off a furious celebration in which teammates surrounded Vini, congratulating him on his effort.[xix]

One might think that having scored the late equalizer, some of Vini's frustrations might have been exorcised. However, being the ultimate competitor that he is, Vini continued to nurse the grudge that he had been developing all match long. Sensing that the match might be getting away from them, Celta Vigo continued to apply maximum pressure on defense, especially when Vinicius came close to a touch on the ball.

In the 86th minute, the referee booked Vini for his second yellow card of the game, this one for diving, and Vini was sent off the field, still furious. Despite the sending-off, it was decidedly apparent that Vini's will to win, as well as his refusal to accept defeat, would play an important role in helping him get to the next level.

Fortunately for Vinicius, Los Blancos supporters, and soccer fans around the world, the opportunity for the young phenom to take his talents to the highest level would be coming sooner rather than later.

Real Madrid 2018-2019

During his time spent primarily at Castilla, Real Madrid made Vinicius available off the bench as a reserve for several games. Vini did not make an appearance during the September 26, 2018, contest, which was a 3-0 defeat on the road at Sevilla FC. Vini saw his first action for Real Madrid during a La Liga home match when he came on as a reserve in the 88th minute, a 0-0 draw with crosstown rivals Atletico Madrid.

Despite only logging two minutes in the contest, the opportunity to play in front of the adoring Los Blanco fans at Bernabeu was a memorable experience. Questioned after the game about his first appearance in a La Liga contest at the iconic stadium, Vini replied, "Right from a young age, I dreamed of playing for Real Madrid, the best team in the world. I'm really grateful for the support from all of the fans. It's a day I'll never forget. There are no words to describe this moment."[xx]

In another interesting historical moment regarding the match, Vinicius' 88th-minute entry into that contest marked the very first time that a player born in the 2000s played an official match for Real Madrid.

The following week, Vinicius also got the opportunity to come off the bench as a replacement, this time in the 80th minute, with the score again knotted at 0-0. Unfortunately for Vini and Madrid, Alaves netted a stoppage-time winner to take the match 1-0.

For Madrid, it was the second straight match in which a statistical record was set. This particular record, however, was not one to be celebrated in the clubhouse or in the press. Madrid's goal-scoring drought now equaled their longest stretch of time without a goal scored in 33 years.[xxi] Thus, the mood among Los Blancos supporters was understandably beginning to sour. Following a disastrous 5-1 defeat at the hands of rivals Barcelona, coach Julen Lopetegui was sacked; the team then turned to the Argentinian Santiago Solari in the hopes that he might be able to correct the course of the season.

With Lopetegui gone, the possibility of a new start under a new manager provided instant benefits for Vini Jr. On October 31, 2018, Vinicius was again called up to the first-team squad—and this time, it would be for good.

In a first-stage match in the Copa del Rey against home-standing UD Melilla, Vini made his first start for the big club, playing all 90 minutes and garnering two assists in a 4-0 dismantling of the overmatched Melilla squad. Returning to Madrid on Nov 3rd, Vinicius once again came off the bench in a 0-0 contest vs Real Valladolid, with new manager Solari hoping that the young Brazilian could inject some life into the listless Madrid squad.

In this instance, Solari's instincts paid off handsomely. Entering the game in the 73rd minute, Vinicius took to the pitch with energy and enthusiasm, making crisp passes and executing sharp runs that had the opponents on their heels. Although officially recorded as an assist, Vinicius cut into the box on the left side and fired a strike which deflected off the keeper for the first goal of the game. A Karim Benzema penalty followed to set the final margin 2-0 in favor of Madrid. The assist was the first goal action for Vinicius in a La Liga contest, and it could not have come at a more opportune time, with his club staring down a six-game stretch without a win in league play.

As the calendar turned to 2019, Real Madrid were starting to round into the kind of form expected of the venerable club. Vini's first La Liga goal for Real Madrid occurred on Feb 3, 2019, in a home match with Alaves. With Madrid clinging to a tenuous 1-0 lead late in the game, Vini directed a ball past the keeper and into the net, giving Madrid some breathing room in an eventual 3-0 victory for the home squad.

The insertion of Vini into the regular rotation brought a breath of life to the club, and the results were starting to make an impact on the league table. The turnaround would be short-lived, however, as two events were about to occur in the following month that would define the season for Los Blancos.

Just as Vinicius was beginning to become a major player in Real Madrid's attacking arsenal, he suffered a season-ending ankle injury during a March 5th UEFA Champions League match against the Dutch powerhouse Ajax. After making a hard run from the midfield spot in the 33rd minute, he experienced a ligament tear near his right ankle and could no longer put weight on the leg, leading him to be replaced. The season-ending injury was a huge personal blow to Vini and a devastating blow to Real Madrid as well.

After losing Vini, Real Madrid endured a stretch of mediocre play. Manager Santiago Solari was sacked on March 11, 2019, after Madrid had been eliminated in both the Copa del Rey and the UEFA Champions League. Stepping in to replace Solari was a familiar face to the club—French soccer legend and former Real Madrid coach Zinedine Zidane.

Although the team responded reasonably well to Zidane's presence on the sideline, Madrid had fallen too far behind in the table, ultimately finishing the season in the third position behind rivals Barcelona and Atletico Madrid. The third-place finish was good enough to earn the club a spot in the UEFA Champions League for the 2019-2020 season, however, and with Zidane's presence back on the sidelines, the future was again looking bright for Real Madrid.

Real Madrid 2019-2020

Although Madrid had initially planned to bring Vinicius along slowly during the previous season, the departure of Cristiano Ronaldo created a vacancy on the left wing, offering the young player an opportunity to accrue much more time on the pitch than originally anticipated. Thanks to this fortuitous turn of events, expectations were high for a fully healthy Vini's second full season with Real Madrid.

Los Blancos loyalists who saw Vini dazzle his opponents with deft dribbling and sharp runs on goal were now having dreams of a dramatically improved Vinicius Jr. in year two, hopefully scoring goals left and right and dishing out assists with clever passes. Given all the hype surrounding Vini's record-setting contract for such a young player and the flashes of brilliance he had shown during the first season before his injury, it was easy to forget that he was also still just a teenager.

But despite being a gifted athlete, Vini still had all the normal worries and emotional maturity issues of a person his age, not to mention the fact that he was still getting used to being thousands of miles away from home and adjusting to the Spanish language and culture. It is in this context that Vini began his second season at Madrid.

Joining Real Madrid that summer were several key new players, including Luka Jovic, Ferland Mendy, Vini's Brazilian countryman Eder Militao, and the young dynamic winger known as Rodrygo. The most impactful summer transfer as it related to Vinicius, however, was left winger Eden Hazard, former Chelsea standout, a Belgian national, and a favorite of manager Zinedine Zidane, who came with a hefty $124MM transfer fee. Given that Vini's preferred position was also at left wing, something of a position battle seemed to be in the offing.

As Hazard's injury status at the beginning of the year kept him from participating in the first few matches of the season, Vinicius had his opening all the same. Starting in three of the first five La Liga contests of the year, Vini collected his first assist and first goal of the season before the end of the first full month of play.

But regardless of this auspicious start to the season, Vinicius soon began to struggle on the pitch, and his playing time became limited as a result. Vini was as proficient as ever with his dribbling and passing, however, his struggles began when it came to shooting the ball. Time after time, Vini had the ball in a position to score but could not seem to deliver a goal.

Coming so close to scoring but failing to deliver was becoming the norm rather than the exception for the struggling young Brazilian. In a 13-game stretch of La Liga contests between mid-September and mid-December 2019, Vinicius was listed as on the bench or not on the squad for 7 of those matches. During the matches that he did participate in, Vini would often be a late substitution or was moved to right wing, a position that he did not prefer. Speculation at the time was that Zidane, who clearly favored Hazard, was taking a "tough love" approach toward Vinicius, thinking that kind of motivation would result in improved form.

Rather than inspiring Vinicius to prove his coach wrong, the benching and position change seemed to have the opposite effect on him. Journalists noted the change in Vini's performance and demeanor. "The relationship with Zidane was clearly difficult," noted one writer at the time. "The Galactico's (Zidane) focus was often on what the youngster needed to do to improve, not on what he did really well. This tough love approach was not necessarily the best for Vini."[v]

All that said, Vini nonetheless showed enough flashes of brilliance to remind Los Blancos supporters why the club had invested so much in him. Vini notched his first UEFA Champions League goal on December 11, 2019, in a contest at Belgian side Club Brugge. In the 64th minute of a 1-1 contest, he collected a pass originally mishandled by Rodrygo and pushed it into the net in what turned out to be the game-winner in a 3-1 victory for Real Madrid.

Another highlight of the season was in the season's second "El Classico," the yearly home matchup with Real Madrid's La Liga rivals Barcelona. On March 1, 2020, in the 71st minute of a scoreless game between first-place Barcelona and second-place Real Madrid, Vinicius unleashed a vicious strike that glanced off a Barca defender, eluding the grasp of the furiously reacting goalkeeper, to notch the first goal of the match. Madrid would go on to add another goal in stoppage time, giving Madrid a 2-0 victory, propelling Los Blancos to the top of the table in the process. Momentum was beginning to build for both Vini and Real Madrid, just in time for the home stretch of the season.

Covid-19 Shutdown

Of course, as the world now knows, shortly after the El Classico competition, La Liga as well as the other professional sporting leagues around the world were forced to pause competition due to the COVID-19 pandemic. On March 12, 2020, La Liga officials determined that matches would be delayed two weeks as a precaution due to the virus. Then, on March 23rd, citing the growing concern over the outbreak of the virus in Spain, La Liga put out a statement declaring that the season would remain on an indefinite hiatus until the Spanish health ministry determined that it would be safe to resume play.[xxii]

While much of the world spent their pandemic time in lockdown streaming shows on television or taking up a new hobby such as experimenting with sourdough bread recipes, Vinicius continued to train and gain strength during this trying period. As fate would have it, Vini's personal trainer one of Brazil's most respected fitness coaches, Thiago Lobo—had been living on-site at Vinicius' home since assisting him in his recovery from his ankle injury during the previous season. As such, Vini could continue to train unimpeded during lockdown, a benefit he took full advantage of.[xxiii]

On May 29, 2020, league officials released a plan for La Liga matches to continue beginning June 11th, with protections in place to limit the spread of COVID-19. Plans called for the season to run through the weekend of July 18-19th, "depending on the evolution" of the virus. Protections to mitigate the spread of the virus included limiting players currently in training to groups of no more than 10, with the objective being to move to full squad training as soon as possible, and more importantly, the matches would be played with no spectators other than team officials and employees allowed in the stadiums.[xxiv]

At the time of the hiatus, Real Madrid sat in second place in the league table, two points behind league leaders Barcelona, with 11 matches remaining. Real Madrid's return to competitive action occurred on June 14, 2020, a home match at the Bernabeu against SD Eibar that resulted in a feel-good 3-1 victory for the home team.

Despite the awkward reboot of the season, Vinicius continued to mostly play the role of the backup for a majority of the matches in the remainder of the season. But after coming off the bench in the first two post-shutdown contests, Vini was back in the starting lineup for consecutive matches on June 21st and June 24th.

In the June 24th contest against home-standing Real Sociedad, Vini provided a key assist by drawing a penalty in the 2-1 victory that saw Madrid rise to the top of the league table. On June 24th, Vinicius took a precision pass from Luca Modric and sent a high chip shot into the net to give Madrid their first goal of the game, which ended in a 2-0 win for the home team, and more importantly, ensuring that their new place as league leaders remained intact.

Real Madrid went on to finish the atypical season in typical fashion, as La Liga champions once again. The 2019-2020 season also saw Madrid win the Spanish Super Cup, although the team fell short in both the quarterfinals of the Copa del Rey and in the Round of 16 of the UEFA Champions League.

For Vinicius, the season marked somewhat of a regression in his performance as compared to his first season with the club. While Vinicius finished the campaign with 5 goals in 38 appearances across all competitions, an increase of 2 goals from the previous year, his assist total decreased to 3.

But perhaps even more worrisome, the Madridistas were beginning to develop concerns about the performance of their new young prodigy. With each failure to convert shots into goals, the narrative was beginning to grow that Vini had a finishing problem. Sure, he could dribble circles around the competition and his instinctive ability to make well-timed runs at the goal were still ever-present, however, Vinicius' inability to convert chances to points clearly vexed both club management as well as the legions of Los Blancos supporters.

Real Madrid 2020-2021

Due to the unplanned hiatus to the previous season and the summer re-start, the 2020-2021 season began in September rather than commencing as usual in August. As the Bernabeu was undergoing structural renovations, Los Blancos' home contests were scheduled to be played in the Alfredo Di Stephano Stadium in Madrid.

Additionally, as COVID-19 was still a factor and protocols continued to be in place, matches were again played in a stadium devoid of supporters. Once again, it was the legendary Frenchman Zinedine Zidane at the helm as Real Madrid prepared to participate in competitions such as the Copa del Rey, the Spanish Super Cup, and the UEFA Champions League as well as the traditional La Liga schedule.

Hoping to leave the disappointments of last season behind him, Vini started the La Liga season in fine form. After playing 90 minutes in a scoreless draw in the season opener and not seeing the field in the second match, the Madridistas were once again shown the explosive brilliance of the young Brazilian. After coming into a scoreless match in the 58th minute of the home opener against Real Valladolid on September 30th, Vinicius made an instant impact on Zinedine Zidane's squad. Battling for possession at the edge of the penalty area, Vini seized the opportunity when the ball bounced off a Valladolid defender and played a strike that eluded the keeper. Best of all, it turned out to be the game-winner in a 1-0 victory.

But when asked about his reaction to his young player's performance, the gaffer was less than effusive in his praise. "I'm happy with the goal and I'm happy with what he did," stated Zidane. "I'm happy in general with the introduction of Marco and Carvajal too. When we make changes, it's to change something, and we did it."[xxv]

Benefitting from the fact that his primary competition at left wing, Eden Hazard, was unavailable to go, Vini got the start in the very next La Liga match on the road against Levante.

Vini wasted little time validating the decision to insert him in the starting lineup, knocking in a shot off a slicing corner kick from Luka Modric to open the scoring. An injury-time finish by Karim Benzema set the final score at 2-0, and Los Blancos' remained unbeaten in the young season.

Vinicius' goal marked the first time he had scored in back-to-back La Liga games in his young career.[xxvi] While the consecutive games with goals certainly buoyed his spirits, the match also showcased some of the same finishing problems that had plagued him since his arrival at Madrid. One instance in particular highlighted this issue, as Vinicius failed to deposit the ball in the mostly empty goal after receiving a brilliant pass from Benzema in the box.

Despite the relatively good start by the squad in the first month of the season, the positive feelings did not last long. Following a 3-2 loss to Shakhtar Donetsk in a first-round UEFA Champions League matchup in which Vini posted a second-half goal, the mood in the locker room began to take a turn for the worse. Players who had fallen out of favor with manager Zinedine Zidane found themselves on the bench, with limited roles for them with the club.

It wasn't just Vinicius that found himself in this position, however. Players who had enjoyed more time on the pitch in the past, such as Isco and Marcello, also suddenly found themselves being passed over in favor of others who had the backing of the coach. In at least one instance, tempers flared when team captain Sergio Ramos confronted Isco regarding his attitude, causing a locker-room confrontation between the two veterans. It was becoming clear that there was a divide among the players, and the team's performance on the pitch reflected as much.

The tension that was brewing in the locker room that fall came to a head at halftime of a UEFA Champions League match on October 27, 2020, on the road at Borussia Monchengladbach. As the players exited the locker room, cameras caught forward Karim Benzema talking to his fellow Frenchman Ferland Mendy, advising him not to share the ball with Vinicius in the second half.

"Don't play with him," Benzema warned Mendy, "I swear on my mother's life he (Vinicius) is playing against us."[xxvii]

Indeed, Benzema refused to play the ball to Vini in the second half of the contest, with Mendy making only the bare minimum of passes to the young Brazilian. The incident naturally became a full-blown controversy, with media reports of the situation becoming widespread, including on television, print media, and all over the internet and social media apps. According to reports, Benzema approached Vinicius the next day to apologize to him and to try to find common ground in hopes of healing the poisonous situation that was developing in the locker room.[xxviii]

Although there continued to be unease amongst the team members, the team started to have more success on the pitch as 2020 was coming to a close. Due to Hazard once again being unavailable because of injury, Vinicius continued to get regular minutes, albeit with uneven results. While the team had climbed back into contention, sitting at second in the table as the year came to a close, Vinicius himself continued a stretch of exhibiting world-class ball-handling skills with below-average finishing ability. During a stretch of games between November 2020 and April 2021, Vinicius recorded only a single goal and accrued just five assists in the process.

The one bright spot remaining for Vinicius in a season filled with struggle was a brilliant performance on April 6, 2021, in the UEFA Champions League quarterfinals against the stronger side from the English Premier League, Liverpool.

With the game nearing the half-hour mark, Vini chased a perfect long ball from Toni Kroos, caught it with his chest, and then fired a strike past the keeper to open the scoring. In doing so, Vini became the second youngest Real Madrid player to score a goal in the knockout stage of the Champions League.[xxix] Although Vini would not be credited with an assist on the second goal, there is no doubt that the pressure that he put on Liverpool's defender Trent Alexander-Arnold caused him to misplay the ball, allowing Marco Asensio to tap the ball past an out of position keeper, thus moving Madrid into a commanding 2-0 lead.

After Liverpool pulled to within a goal following a splendid strike from celebrated Egyptian attacker Mo Salah, the stage was set for even more magic from the young Brazilian. In the 65th minute of play, midfielder Luka Modric rolled a perfect cross that found Vini's feet, allowing the Brazilian to put the ball through a defender's leg and off the body of the goalkeeper, setting the final score at 3-0 in favor of Real Madrid.

Despite finishing a close second in the La Liga standings and once again earning a place in the following year's UEFA Champions League, Real Madrid finished the season without winning a single trophy for the first time since the 2009-2010 season.

For Vinicius Jr., the 2020-2021 season marked the third-straight campaign in which he did not fully meet the expectations of the club or the Los Blancos supporters. In 49 matches, including all appearances, Vinicius netted only six goals and seven assists. Even worse for Vini, a narrative was beginning to take place that Madrid had overpaid for the young Brazilian. Although he could dribble circles around defenders with regularity, he was earning a reputation as a player who all too frequently could not finish the ultimate job of putting the ball in the net.

So, if Vinicius was going to change the narrative, he would have to do it soon. Otherwise, he faced the risk of being labeled a bust before he even reached the age of 21.

Real Madrid 2021-2022

The disappointing conclusion to the previous season led to some significant off-field changes for Real Madrid. The first was the abrupt resignation of head coach Zinedine Zidane, which was actually his second time calling it quits as Madrid's head man. Of course, as the relationship between Vinicius and Zidane was anything but harmonious, a new gaffer could have been just the thing the young Brazilian needed to re-boot his struggling career.

Within days of Zidane's departure, Real Madrid settled on bringing back one of the most successful managers in the club's history, Carlo Ancelotti. When asked at his introductory press conference about his thoughts about Vinicius, Ancelotti replied that he had a lot of faith in the young player, and that he would be given his fair share of chances to succeed.[xxx]

Although Vini was eager to show off his talent for the new coach, when the La Liga season began in August 2021, he continued to be in his customary role from the previous seasons—coming off the bench as a second-half substitution.

While remaining in this lesser role to begin the new season might have been demoralizing for many young players, perhaps even a reason to dial back the effort or to quit trying altogether, it seems like the opposite was true for Vinicius. Entering the season-opening game on the road to Alaves in the 66th minute, Vinicius banged home the final goal of a 4-1 victory.

Similarly, in the second La Liga game one week later at Levante, Vinicius entered the game in the 59th minute with his club on the short end of a 2-1 score. In the 70th minute, Vini took a through ball from teammate Casemiro and slotted the ball past the keeper to level the score at 2-2. After Levante took advantage of some sloppy defensive work to regain the lead, it was again time for Vinicius to demonstrate his improved finishing skills. In the 84th minute with his team trailing by a goal, Vinicius took a shot in the box from a tight angle, glancing it off the post and into the goal to set the final score at 3-3, earning a point for his team.

Given his performances in the first two La Liga contests, optimism was growing from all corners of Los Blancos nation that perhaps this was the year for Vinicius to finally make his mark and fulfill the promise that fans had only seen heretofore in glances. A local Madridistas blog wondered aloud if Vini's finishing woes had ceased to be.

Posing the question of whether Vini had found his mojo in the box, the writers offered, "His two goals were not good, they were excellent. He has scored three goals in just two games off the bench. If he can play with this confidence, the sky is the limit."[xxxi] Journalist Jorge Valdano echoed this sentiment by declaring on live TV, "Vinicius has learned how to finish in a week!"[v]

Naturally, Vinicius' hot start to the new season was not lost on Ancelotti. Thanks to Vini's excellent performance as a substitute during the first two matches of the season, the gaffer slotted him into the starting lineup beginning with the third game.

Now given the opportunity to start as a reward for his improved form, Vinicius did not disappoint. Through the first six La Liga contests of the young season, Vini compiled five goals and three assists, which was two more goals than he had in the full La Liga season in the year prior! As a result, the team sprinted out of the gate with five wins and one draw.

So, how does one explain the sudden confidence and dramatically improved finishing ability displayed by the young Vinicius Jr. to begin the 2021-2022 campaign?

Certainly, age and experience had to be major factors in this turnaround. It makes sense that his continued adjustment to a new culture and the sudden, worldwide fame had played roles, along with the fact that he was simply maturing from a boy to a man. Part of the reason for Vinicius' innate ability to endure the difficult stretches and persevere when others might have folded could lie in his personality and the strength of his national heritage as well.

As his Brazil U-17 coach Carlos Amadeu noted, "Vinicius is a typical *Carioca* (person from Rio)—extroverted, talkative, someone who loves to have fun and mess about." Of Vinicius' personality, Amadeu added, "He's a happy kid. And he also has a strong personality: he overcomes difficulties with ease, faces challenges head-on, and can live with the demands and the expectations placed upon him."[v]

But perhaps the most influential piece of the puzzle that finally allowed Vini Jr. to turn things around for himself was the support of his new coach. While Zidane's focus had always been on what the young player was doing wrong, Ancelotti's much more positive approach was to augment what Vini was already doing well and make minor tweaks to put him in better opportunities to succeed.

To that end, Ancelotti began working directly with Vini on getting him to take earlier shots and limit his number of touches near the box. Ancelotti also began to adjust tactics to make it easier for Vinicius to move into open spaces on the counterattack.[v]

As the days grew shorter and the cool returned to the air in the fall of 2021, Ancelotti had worked his magic; Madrid was sitting atop the La Liga standings and was making waves in the UEFA Champions League matches as well.

Vinicius scored two goals and garnered one assist in a 5-0 October victory over Shakhtar Donetsk in a group-stage competition in the Champions League. Then, returning to La Liga play on November 28th, Vinicius displayed incredible finishing ability in the 89th minute of a 1-1 game. After reining in a long pass off his chest, he eluded several defenders with skillful dribbling and then landed a shot from 25 yards away. It was the pivotal score that earned his club a clutch win over third-place Sevilla.

With Vini now rounding into form and enjoying the full backing of his coaches, Vini's teammates had also become more confident in his ability to put the ball in the goal. This was evident when team leader and talisman Karim Benzema began to include him in his attacking patterns. Indeed, one of the hallmarks of the 2021-2022 season was Vinicius assisting on Benzema's goals.

Nowhere was this seen more clearly than in the knockout rounds of the UEFA Champions League. In the second leg of the Round of 16 contest at home against Kylian Mbappe, Lionel Messi, and their mates at Paris Saint-Germain, Vinicius pressured the PSG goalkeeper into making an error. This allowed him to collect a scattershot clearance and shuttle the ball to Benzema, thus tying the game in the second half of an eventual 3-1 series-clinching victory. Lightning would strike again in the quarterfinal round versus a seasoned Chelsea squad, as Vinicius assisted a Benzema goal on both legs, sending Madrid through to the next round.

Of course, no story about Vinicius' 2022 UEFA Champions League exploits would be complete without mentioning his incredible performance in the Champions League final. After dispatching Manchester City in the semifinals on a 6-5 aggregate score that saw Vinicus garner a first-leg goal, the stage was set for a Champions League final rematch vs transcendent talent Mo Salah and Liverpool. After Real Madrid's victory in the 2018 Champions League finals, Liverpool and their legendary manager Jurgen Klopp were keen to avenge their loss.

After a scoreless first half that saw a few chances for scoring elude each team, Real Madrid goalkeeper Thibaut Courtois made an extraordinary save by punching the ball away from an incoming header attempt by a Liverpool attacker. The stage was then set for the kind of drama befitting the most prestigious tournament in European soccer. In the 59th minute, Vinicius Jr. collected a low cross from teammate Frederico Valverde at the edge of the 18-yard box and fired it into the goal behind a Liverpool keeper, providing the game-winner and only score of the contest.

The 2021-2022 season was a great success for both Vini and the team as a whole. In addition to winning the UEFA Champions League title, Madrid also finished at the top of the La Liga table, 13 points clear of second-place Barcelona. Ancelotti and company also added another Spanish Super Cup title along the way, securing a domestic double title in the process. For Vinicius, the 2021-2022 season was his breakout campaign. Across all competitions, he played in 52 matches, scoring 22 goals and contributing 20 assists in the process.

Given the significance of the season's turnaround and Vinicius's much-improved play, a deeper dive into his performance is certainly warranted to determine why he was able to put it all together on the pitch in the 2021-2022 campaign.

The most notable difference, and certainly the one that will get the most attention was Vinicius' ability to finish in the box and score at an impressive clip. With the backing of the experienced Ancelotti, Vini appeared to be more relaxed in matches, not fearing that a single mistake was going to lead to his being replaced. A more relaxed player is a more confident player, and a more confident player is calmer with the ball and relies on the combination of natural ability and learned technical and tactical skill to carry the day.

A second and often overlooked aspect of Vini's improved form was his commitment to being an all-around player, not just a scorer. During the 2021-2022 season, Vini displayed an improved ability to track back on defense and assist other players on defense, thus becoming a strategic part of getting the deadly Real Madrid counterattack started. Knowing that they were not solely responsible for all the defensive heavy lifting allowed the left and center backs for Los Blancos more room for creativity in defending as well as in attacking. Vini's more relaxed approach contributed to him being a more effective defender as well, allowing him to put pressure on the opposition and recover the ball cleanly while lowering the chances of committing a costly penalty.[xxxii]

In the span of just a year, the narrative around Vinicius Jr. changed from that of a talented player who did not seem capable of consistently playing at his potential to being regarded as one of the best and most reliable scorers in world soccer. The challenge to come for the young star was to now prove that his breakout performance was not just an aberration but rather a harbinger of continued future success.

Real Madrid 2022-2023

Each new season is eagerly anticipated by supporters of the world's most famous soccer team. On the heels of tumultuous or less-than-stellar campaigns, the faithful Madristas ride a wave of optimism that the problems of the previous year would be addressed and that better days were to come. Following successful campaigns, the fanbase is full of hopes and dreams of sustaining good form and once again bringing home the spoils of victory in trophies and individual awards for their beloved Galacticos.

The latter was certainly the case when it came to Real Madrid supporters entering the 2022-2023 season. Not only was the team defending champions of both La Liga and the UEFA Champions League, but now, with two legitimate Ballon d'Or contenders in Benzema and Vinicius, odds were also good for a repeat performance from Madrid.

For the first time in years, there appeared to be a solid foundation within the coaching ranks as well, as Carlo Ancelotti was returning to the sidelines once again to lead the team for the upcoming fixtures. Despite the departures of longtime Real Madrid standouts Marcelo, Casemiro, Gareth Bale, and Luka

Jovic, the team added notable defender Antonio Rudiger and midfielder Aurelien Tchouameni to the squad.

After a pre-season trip to the United States for a run of three international friendlies, the squad opened their season with a victory over Eintracht Frankfurt in the UEFA Super Cup, a match which saw Vinicius assist Benzema's second-half goal to secure a 2-0 win and another trophy for the club.

The early successes continued with the beginning of La Liga league play, as Madrid began the season undefeated in the first 12 matches. Following the same script as the previous season, it was Vinicius and Benzema leading the way for Los Blancos. Over the course of the unbeaten streak, Vinicius collected six goals and two assists, continuing his run of fine form established in the previous season.

Similarly, the club started fast right out of the gate at the beginning of Champions League play that fall. In the group stage of competition, Real Madrid breezed through the competition, finishing in first place in the group and advancing to the knockout stage once again. With a combined four goals and one assist in the group stage, Vinicius led the team in goals scored, proving to any remaining doubters that he had conquered the pesky finishing problems that once menaced him at the beginning of his tenure in Madrid.

In fact, it appeared that the only thing that could stop Vini's momentum at the time was the halting of La Liga play following the matches of November 10th to accommodate players competing for their countries in the 2022 FIFA World Cup in Qatar. Vinicius set off to compete for Brazil having participated in 21 matches across all competitions, securing 10 goals and 5 assists and leading his team to second place in La Liga, just 2 points off the pace of rival Barcelona.

Following the international break, Vinicius and his Real Madrid comrades returned to La Liga play as well as competitions in the Copa del Rey and Spanish Super Cup tournaments, with the FIFA Club World Cup looming as well. Despite a loss in the Spanish Super Cup final to bitter rival Barcelona in January, Vinicius and Madrid continued to battle in the other January fixtures.

Getting off to a strong start in the Copa del Rey, Madrid had little trouble in the early rounds, breezing into the semi-finals with an unblemished record. Additionally, Los Blancos continued to take care of league business, staying within striking distance of the league leaders.

As winter was giving way to spring, Vinicius and his Real Madrid mates continued to rank below Catalan rivals Barcelona on the La Liga table. Although their play brimmed with creativity and crisp execution at times, such as the 4-0 Copa del Rey semifinal dismantling of the Catalans in Barcelona in which Vinicius scored a goal and supplied two assists, the team also had some baffling, lackluster performances in which they dropped points to seemingly inferior opponents. Despite Vinicius' consistent run of fine form, Los Blancos could not overtake Barcelona in the La Liga table, instead settling for a second-place finish, a full 10 points behind their bitter rivals.

Despite their failure to repeat as La Liga champions, Real Madrid's already bulging trophy cabinet increased by three over the course of the season. The squad emerged victorious in the Copa del Rey, UEFA Super Cup, and the FIFA Club World Cup competitions.

For the second consecutive year, Vinicius' individual statistics were an accurate reflection of his potential on the pitch. Across 55 appearances in all competitions, the up-and-coming Brazilian compiled 23 goals and 21 assists. For his efforts, Vinicius was selected as La Liga's Player of the Year, further cementing his growing reputation as one of the best football players in the world.

Turning Points

When surveying the entirety of Vinicius' performance during the 2022-2023 season, two events stand out above the rest. The first of these occurred on February 21, 2023, in a UEFA Champions League Round of 16 match against familiar Premier League foe, Jurgen Klopp's Liverpool Reds.

Despite Liverpool's recent run of domestic and European league successes, their recent history going against Real Madrid left a lot to be desired. Fresh off the previous year's Champions League final in which Vinicius provided the only score of the match, the squads were once again facing each other in the most glamourous of European club soccer competitions. Also similar to the match in 2022, Vinicius Jr. would have a notable influence on the outcome of the match.

The contest could not have started more prosperously for Liverpool, as they pushed across the first score of the game in just the fourth minute. Then, almost inconceivably, Thibaut Courtois, the remarkable Madrid goalkeeper, made a costly mistake. The normally sure-handed Courtois mishandled a routine ball, sending it to the pitch directly at the feet of the sensational Liverpool attacker Mo Salah, who calmly deposited the ball into the net.

Disaster was looming for Real Madrid. They were down 2-0 in the first leg of the Round of 16, and now faced the daunting task of salvaging their UEFA hopes in front of a crowd of raucous Liverpudlians who were eager to see Los Blancos go down. But while Real Madrid supporters were seeing calamity unfold before their eyes, Vinicius saw something else—an opportunity to write his name in the history books next to the pantheon of Los Blancos greats by sparking an unbelievable comeback.

It started innocently enough, with the experienced Madrid side refusing to cave to the moment as they stuck to their game plan of executing crisp passes and finding players in space. A near miss occurred in the 20th minute as a low cross from Rodrygo barely eluded the reach of a streaking Karim Benzema in the box.

Then, it was time for Vini to exert his will upon the contest. In the 21st minute, Vinicius made a quick cut into the box from the left wing, sending the ball to Benzema as he ran. Benzema then returned the ball to Vini, who continued his run to the goal, uncorked a shot in heavy traffic that eluded the Liverpool goalkeeper, and neatly cut the Liverpool advantage to just one.

Then, it was the normally reliable Liverpool goalkeeper Alisson Becker's chance to commit a significant and costly blunder.

Looking to play a ball tapped back to him by a Liverpool defender in the 36th minute, Becker nonchalantly kicked the ball in the direction of an onrushing Vinicius, who was attempting to apply pressure to the keeper in hopes of forcing a mistake. Vinicius' hustle paid off, as Becker's ill-advised pass caromed off the onrushing Brazilian, landing behind the bewildered keeper and bouncing into the goal, leveling the tally at 2-2. The Liverpool crowd, who less than five minutes prior had been in the throes of soccer revelry, were now stunned into silence as Vini slid on his knees in celebration following the score.

After exiting the dressing rooms for the second half with the score knotted at 2-2, it did not take long for Vinicius to once again dictate the flow of the game. Following a brilliant display of dribbling and eluding several defenders, Vini was taken down just outside of the penalty area, winning a free kick for Real Madrid. The experienced Luka Modric took the kick, placing a superb ball into the six-yard box where it was headed home by Eder Militao, giving Real Madrid their first lead of the game at 3-2. Then, a 55th-minute goal by team talisman Karim Benzema extended the Real Madrid lead to 4-2, and the visitors finally had some breathing room.

But Vini Jr. was far from finished rubbing salt in the wounds of the Anfield spectators that day. After a clever defensive effort from Modric, stealing the ball near midfield and starting a counterattack, Modric rushed up-field, spotting Vinicius rushing down the left wing toward the goal. The highly decorated veteran Croatian played the ball ahead to Vinicius, who made a brilliant short pass between two retreating defenders to the feet of Benzema just outside of the box. Taking three small touches, Benzema eluded both the onrushing keeper and two Liverpool defenders, then guided the ball into the far corner, scoring the final goal of the improbable comeback as Real Madrid won the first leg of the Round of 16 by a score of 5-2.

Vini's spectacular performance in the match, scoring two goals and contributing to two more, was a prime example of the caliber of play he had been exhibiting over the past two seasons. Skillful passing, deft dribbling, and confident finishing were now the norm for the young star, who was finally proving his detractors wrong.

Despite Real Madrid bowing out of the Champions League semifinal round to eventual champion Manchester City, the team had enjoyed a very bountiful year. Employing a successful mix of veteran stalwarts in Toni Kroos, Luka Modric, and Thibaut Courtois with young up-and-coming rising stars in

Vinicius Jr., Rodrygo, and Frederico Valverde, the squad seemed destined for more trophies in the near future.

Vinicius Encounters Racist Abuse

In a reminder that the world of international soccer is situated within the larger world full of division and grievances, the issue of racism in sports became front and center in La Liga competitions in 2023, with Vinicius Jr. bearing the brunt of the vile racist assaults.

Prior to a much-anticipated Madrid Derby clash with Atletico Madrid in January 2023, an effigy of Vinicius Jr. was hung over a highway in an act of blatant racism. Although it was hardly the first time that a black athlete was the target of derisive abuse, the shocking nature and high visibility of the action caused an international stir.

While the league condemned the action and promised legal action against those involved in the disgusting act, many saw the response of La Liga officials as a half-hearted effort that was insufficient in protecting players against similar actions in the future. In the absence of a cohesive strategy by the league to address the problem, Vinicius continued to be the target of racist chants and actions that spring. According to an account by ESPN, Vinicius encountered racist abuse in February during contests at Osasuna and Mallorca, and in March matches at Barcelona and Real Betis.[xxxiii]

By the time the away match against Valencia rolled around on May 21, 2023, Vinicius had reached his breaking point. In the 73rd minute of a tense match, with his squad on the short side of a 1-0 deficit, Real Madrid midfielder Toni Kroos was preparing to take a free kick near the box. As Kroos was lining up for the set piece, Vinicius could be seen gesturing toward the crowd behind the goal, responding to racist shouts directed at him.

As players from both sides attempted to pull Vinicius away from the offending spectators, Vinicius continued to hold firm in his response. Pointing at individual spectators in the stands, Vini hotly attested, "He called me a monkey!"[xxxiii]

Madrid teammates jumped to his defense, countering the chants with profanity-laden shouts directed at the racists in the crowd. The head referee then entered into the fray, and after separating the players, instituted the "anti-racism" protocol, during which the match was temporarily halted and reminders to the crowd were made via the public address speakers that further racist statements would result in expulsion from the stadium.

Following the match, Vinicius took to social media to further express his outrage at continuing to be targeted by such vile statements and behavior. In a lengthy statement, Vini said, "It wasn't the first time, nor the second, nor the third. Racism is normal in La Liga. The competition thinks it's normal, the Federation does too, and the opponents encourage it. I'm so sorry. The championship that once belonged to Ronaldinho, Ronaldo, Cristiano, and Messi is now that of racists. A beautiful nation, which welcomed me and which I love, but which agreed to export the image of a racist country to the world. I'm sorry for the Spaniards who don't agree, but today, in Brazil, Spain is known as a country of racists. And, unfortunately, because of everything that happens every week, I can't defend it. I agree. But I am strong, and I will go to the end against racists. Even if far from here."[xxxiv]

Since the events of May 2023, La Liga officials have taken some steps to address the problem of racist abuse of players. The people responsible for hanging the effigy in Madrid were arrested and would go to trial for their actions. Plus, La Liga has introduced an initiative aimed at preventing racist abuse through an education campaign.

Yet, despite these efforts, these problems have continued to surface, and many people continue to criticize La Liga for not implementing stricter penalties on teams whose fans engage in racist behaviors from the stands. Many others, such as Spanish activist Moha Gerehou, argue that more should be done to punish individual teams for the behavior of their fans. Gerehou has suggested that teams should lose points in the standings, or that the clubs should have to forfeit the gate receipts if they cannot eliminate the racist chants and gestures of their fans.[xxxv]

It is unclear if any of these approaches or a combination of several of them will make a substantial difference in the mistreatment of La Liga players of color. What is clear, however, is that while Vinicius did not seek the position as point person to call out La Liga officials for their failure to adequately address the problem of racism in their sport, he remains willing and most certainly able to be one of the loudest voices in the fight.

Chapter 3: International Career

While many professional soccer players relish individual accolades and club trophies are celebrated with appropriate pomp and circumstance, it is often the case that the highest honor and achievement for any player is to wear the jersey of their home country in international competitions.

This is certainly true for Vinicius Jr. The charismatic and patriotic Brazilian footballer is now a bona fide superstar in his homeland. It should be noted that soccer is followed with religious fervor in Brazil, and while the professional clubs throughout the South American country certainly have their devoted fanbases, Brazilians save their most rabid and high-octane energy for the highly decorated Brazilian national team.

Alternately referred to as *The Seleção* (The Selection) or *The Canarinha* (Little Canary), the colors of the team dressed in bright yellow, blue, and green can be seen on Brazilians young and old all across the country. Winners of a record five World Cups, Brazil is home to some of the best players in the history of international football.

Of course, any discussion of soccer greats has to begin with the Brazilian-born Pele, known by many as the greatest player ever to play the game. But no list of other notable Brazilian stars of the past is complete without also mentioning greats such as Garrincha, Ronaldo, Zico, and Romario. Today, Brazil continues to be represented by some of the brightest stars in the game. This includes Vinicius Jr., Gabriel Jesus, Ederson, Gabriel Martinelli, Alisson, Matheus Cunha, Richarlison, and Casemiro.

Brazil U-15, U-17, and U-20

Vinicius' involvement with the Brazilian national team began when he was selected to the Brazil U-15 squad in October 2015, just in time for the South American Under 15 Championships.

Vini's first goal wearing his country's jersey came on November 26, 2015, in a 6-1 victory over Peru. Feeling the confidence of his first score for his country, young Vini added two more goals in a 3-0 victory over Bolivia just two days later. If Vinicius was feeling any nervousness in competing for his country, it was not on display during the U-15 competitions. The youngster was performing like a seasoned veteran, exhibiting deft ball control, executing pinpoint passes, and making exhilarating goal-scoring runs down the field.

On December 6, 2015, Vinicius and his Brazilian teammates faced a talented Uruguay squad in the championship match of the tournament. At the conclusion of a scoreless draw in the final, Vini and company emerged as champions with a 5-4 penalty shootout in a dramatic finish. As a result of his inspired play, Vinicius was named the tournament's Most Valuable Player, finishing with a team-second six goals in the competition, one behind the team leader. In 10 appearances for the U-15 squad, Vinicius compiled an impressive seven total goals across 10 appearances in all competitions.

In June 2016, Vinicius was invited to join the Brazilian U-17 squad in preparation for a friendly against Chile. Still only 15 years old at the time, young Vini outplayed his older competitors, scoring two goals and assisting in two others, contributing to all four goals in a 4-2 victory. On the heels of this performance, Vini was selected for Brazil's 2017 South American Cup U-17 competition, held in Chile.

Vinicius wasted no time in making his presence felt, as he scored his team's first goal of the competition only 13 minutes into the first match versus Peru, in an eventual 3-0 win for the Brazilian side. Not content to rest on his laurels, Vini continued to lead the Brazil squad to the first-place finish at the end of the group stage of the competition.

As the tournament continued, Vinicius picked right up where he left off, notching braces in back-to-back matches against

Ecuador and Colombia. Moving into the final round of the competition, Brazil faced the home-standing Chile squad with the trophy, and more importantly, national pride, on the line. Despite going goalless in the final, Vinicius played a critical role in securing the title, leading his team to a 5-0 rout of Chile.

Vinicius finished the competition with a total of seven goals and two assists in eight games. For his efforts, Vinicius was once again named the MVP in the tournament. In total, Vinicius competed in 15 contests with the U-17 squad, scoring 13 goals and contributing 2 assists, proving his readiness for the next challenge.

Before joining the top-flight Brazilian National team in international competitions, Vinicius logged two performances for the national U-20 team. Suiting up for the U-20 team in October 2018, Vini helped his team achieve draws in successive friendly matches against the Chilean U-20 squad. Vinicius assisted the lone Brazilian goal in a 1-1 draw, playing the entire 90 minutes of the match. Although not reaching the scoring column in the second game, Vini supplied aggressive defense, coming on as a reserve in the 2-2 draw.

Brazil First Team

Given his performance on the pitch for Brazil's younger squads, it was only a matter of time before Vinicius would get the call to join the Brazil national squad's first team. That call came in February 28, 2019, just in time for the upcoming friendly competitions scheduled against Panama and the Czech Republic.

The timing appeared to be just right for Vinicius, as he was also beginning to come into form for Real Madrid, having recently earned more playing time and positive coverage in the press. The exhilaration he must have felt at the call-up proved to be short-lived, however, as the young winger suffered a torn ankle ligament several days later in a UEFA Champions League match.

Despite his return to play with Madrid and the public clamor for him to be included, he was left out of the Brazilian squad for the 2019 Copa America competition.[xxxvi] Regardless of Vinicius' absence from the squad, however, Brazil emerged victorious in the tournament, defeating runner up Peru by an impressive 3-1 margin.

Fully healed from his spring ankle injury, Vinicius finally got the opportunity for his first senior team cap (the soccer term for a player representing his country in an international appearance), on September 11, 2019, in a friendly competition held in Los Angeles against rival South American squad Peru. Wearing jersey No. 19, Vinicius entered the match in the 72nd minute and played the remainder of what would become a 1-0 defeat to the Peruvian side.

As the calendar turned to 2020, the Brazilian national team began to participate in qualification matches in advance of the 2022 FIFA World Cup. Vinicius was selected to remain with the senior team for these matches, which began in the fall of 2020. Although healthy and ready to contribute, Vini did not appear in either of Brazil's qualification wins against Venezuela and Uruguay that fall. Similarly, Vinicius did not make an appearance in the May 2021 qualification wins against Paraguay and Ecuador.

Fortunately for young Vinicius, his patience paid off as he earned his Copa America appearance in the first game of the group stage on June 13, 2021. Making the moment even sweeter, Vini was also making his first international appearance in front of his legion of fans, as the competition was hosted by Brazil. Coming on in the 85th minute, Vini played the remainder of a 3-0 win over Venezuela.

Following a similar trend, Vinicius entered three additional Copa America matches as a second-half substitute over the course of June and July 2021. Although he did not garner any goals or assists during the competition, Vinicius arguably gained something even more valuable. Taking the pitch for his country, Vini was able to work his way into the rotation with no expectations of grandeur, as the team featured several accomplished international players who shouldered much of the burden for the home-standing Brazilians. Despite a strong overall performance by the team, Brazil would have to settle for second place, losing a hard-fought 1-0 defeat at the hands of Lionel Messi's Argentinian squad.

By the end of 2021, the preparation for the 2022 World Cup was kicking into high gear. Fortunately for Vinicius, he was becoming a larger part of the plans for coach Adenor "Tite" Leonardo Bacchi's Brazilian national team. Additionally, Vinicius was beginning to be included in the starting lineup, penciled in as the left wing attacker in World Cup qualifying matches.

Tite's confidence in his young phenom proved well placed, as Vinicius finally broke into the scoring column for the first time in international competition, providing the second goal in a 4-0 victory over Chile in Rio de Janeiro. Perhaps even more critical for Brazil's World Cup prospects, however, was the addition of a healthy and in-form Vini, now paired with his Real Madrid teammate Rodrygo and the celebrated Brazilian icon Neymar Jr., all of whom formed a fearsome attacking force behind the inspired play of striker Richarlison, of the Premier League's formidable Tottenham Hotspur.

The *Seleçaõ Brasileira* were finally starting to click on all cylinders, just in time for the world's biggest sporting spectacle, the FIFA World Cup.

2022 FIFA World Cup

The 2022 edition of the beautiful game's grandest stage took place in the desert kingdom of Qatar. The contests were scheduled for November and December 2022, moved from the more traditional summertime placement to accommodate the blast-furnace summers of the Middle East.

Going into the tournament, Brazil was widely seen as the odds-on favorite to emerge victorious at +350, ahead of the likes of international powerhouses Argentina (+500), England (+700), and defending champions France (+700).[xxxvii] Despite Brazil's record five World Cup trophies, the country's recent run of play in the grandest of competitions had left a lot to be desired. It had been 20 years since Brazil had been at the top of the international soccer world, and the bitter taste of Brazil's shocking 7-1 home-turf defeat by the Germans in the 2014 FIFA World Cup still lingered large in the psyche of the Seleçaõ faithful.

Still, despite the recent years of substandard performances by their lofty standards, many Brazilians believed that 2022 was going to be the year of the "Hexa," meaning the sixth FIFA World Cup title for their cherished national team. Thus, the mood on the streets of Rio De Janeiro and Saõ Paulo, as well as in the countless smaller cities and towns across Brazil, was one of optimism. The canary yellow, blue, and green of the national team's iconic kits could be seen on the young, the old, and everyone in between in this football-crazed country. For a nation fractured with unrest and warring political factions, soccer, and especially World Cup soccer, was a much-needed and welcome reprieve.

In the words of Hemerson Cabral, a 35-year-old janitor from Saõ Paulo, the country undergoes a type of metamorphosis during the World Cup. "When Brazil are playing, many people finish work so they get back home earlier to watch it with the family or with the neighbors," he reported, later indicating that the Brazilians would eventually emerge victorious over the reigning champions, France. "They (France) are the only obstacle. It will be a great match and Brazil will win. The atmosphere at Brazil matches is second to none. I don't think there are football fans like us. We enter the pitch with the players."[xxxviii]

With the hopes and dreams of their countrymen and women riding on their shoulders, the Brazilians boarded the jet to Qatar that November with dreams of bringing home the Hexa for their devoted fans. Why wouldn't they? With their formidable front-line attack bolstered by the daring midfield presence in the likes of Casemiro and Fred, the defensive stalwarts Marquinhos and team captain Thiago Silva, and the incomparable goalkeeper Ederson, the sky was seemingly the limit for this conglomeration of seasoned veterans and skillful newcomers.

With the wait finally over, Vinicius and his Brazilian teammates took to the pitch for their first match versus Serbia in the group stage of the 2022 FIFA World Cup on November 24, 2022. As had been customary over the past few months, Vini found himself in the starting lineup at left wing, playing alongside one of his childhood heroes, Neymar Jr.

Any thinking that the Serbian side would roll over and easily capitulate to the superior Brazilian squad certainly was vanquished by the spirited play of the Serbians in the scoreless first half. Brazilian striker Richarlison finally got the first score of the game, easily directing a deflected ball in the back of the net from the six-yard box to give Brazil the lead. Minutes later, Vinicius found Richarlison in nearly the identical location in the box, firing a cross that caused the striker to instinctively rear back and fire the ball past the keeper with a dazzling scissor kick that sent the Brazilian fans into delirium. Although it was not the walk in the park that many had expected, Brazil nevertheless emerged from their initial contest with a 2-0 victory. Logging 75 minutes and assisting on the second goal, Vinicius Jr. was proving that he belonged on the world of sports' biggest stage.

Buoyed by their win in the first match of group stage, Brazil then went on to earn a win in the second-round match against Switzerland, despite Neymar Jr. not being able to play due to injury. With Neymar unavailable, Tite adjusted his tactics, employing a 4-4-3 formation that saw Vini, Richarlison, and Raphinha on the front line. The change in strategy was effective, as Brazil once again escaped with a harder-than-anticipated victory, this time, 1-0 over the Swiss.

Having already secured a place in the knockout stage due to wins in the first two contests, Tite then decided to rest many of his regular starters, Vinicius included, for the next match against Cameroon. The second squad battled Cameroon impressively, eventually falling to the African club 1-0 after a stoppage-time goal before the final whistle. Despite the meaningless loss, the Brazilians were moving on, where a veteran squad from South Korea and their captain, Premier League standout Son Heung-min, awaited them in the Round of 16 knockout stage contest.

The South Korean side was entering the contest with renewed hopes, fresh off a victory over Cristiano Ronaldo's Portugal squad in the group stage. The Brazilians were also encouraged by the return of star Neymar Jr. to the lineup following his injury. With this as the background, both teams had reasons for optimism in the win-or-go-home knockout round.

In a nearly reverse form from the horrendous 7-1 World Cup thrashing in 2014 by the Germans, it was the Brazilians who this time charged out of the gate from the opening whistle. With Brazil back to their customary 4-2-3-1 formation, Vinicius took a clever Raphinha cross from the opposite side of the box in the seventh minute of action and somehow steered the ball past three South Korean defenders and into the goal, staking the Brazilians to an early 1-0 lead. Almost before the crowd stopped cheering the first goal, Richarlison drew a foul in the box, setting up a second goal via penalty kick from Neymar Jr.

With the South Korean side seemingly stunned and disorganized, the Brazilians continued their aggressive start. A 29th-minute goal from Richarlison put Brazil ahead 3-0, and the rout was on. If there was any doubt that Brazil could sustain their offensive outburst and put the game out of reach, Vinicius surely answered that in the 36th minute. Spotting Raphinha as he made his way into the box, Vinicius lofted a nifty cross from the left side that landed perfectly at his teammate's feet, allowing him to tap it in for the score, putting Brazil on the glide path to victory. South Korea managed to avoid the shutout with a score in the 79th minute, but it was too little too late. Brazil was moving on to the quarterfinals on the heels of a 4-1 dismantling of the talented Asian side.

Moving on to the quarterfinals, Brazil would next face European powers Croatia, led by the sensational Luka Modric, winner of the 2018 Ballon d'Or as the best soccer player of the year. Vinicius and Rodrygo, no strangers to their Real Madrid teammate Modric's outstanding play, were fully aware of his ability to impact the game on both ends of the pitch. Meanwhile, Croatia, fresh off their loss in the 2018 finals, were in search of their first World Cup championship.

Held in the city of Al Rayyan, the match saw the two talented and experienced sides engaged in an epic battle, with the

Brazilians having the advantage in shots on goal but neither team managing to score in regular time. Having started the game at left wing, Vinicius was removed from the game in the 64th minute for defensive reasons, as he was repeatedly tested and beaten by the speedy Croatian attackers.

The match remained scoreless until injury minutes at the end of the first period of extra time, when Neymar Jr. fired a close-range shot at an impossibly steep angle that bounced off of the roof of the net, giving Brazil a 1-0 lead with 15 minutes left to play. Unfortunately for the Brazilians, a defensive lapse ensured that their lead would be short-lived.

With a mere three minutes standing between Brazil and a date in the semi-finals with Leo Messi's Argentina, disaster struck. A Luka Modric ball found a streaking Mislav Orsic, who was racing down the left touchline toward the goal. Orsic collected the ball, steered it into the box, and then deftly passed it slightly backward to a waiting Bruno Petrovic, who sent the ball flying past the Brazilian keeper to level the game at 1-1. As the remaining minutes ticked off the clock, ensuring that the game would be decided by penalty kicks, Brazilian fans were left wondering what had happened. They were so close to victory, only to have their hearts snatched by cruel fate once again!

Inspired by their miraculous, defeat-defying goal in the closing minutes of extra time, the momentum was clearly with the Croatians as the teams lined up for the penalty kicks to determine who would be moving on to the semi-finals. As Vinicius had been taken off the field for a substitute during regulation, he was unable to participate in the high-stakes shootout. The penalty kick drama unfolded like a Croatian dream, as the Brazilians were behind from the get-go, missing their first attempt while each successive Croatian player calmly knocked their shots home with ease.

With the tally at four made goals to two, Brazil's hopes were squarely on the shoulders of vice-captain Marquinhos as he stepped up to the ball in a make-or-go-home moment. Marquinhos sent a low howling line drive ball off the post, but it ricocheted back onto the field of play and away from the goal, setting off a frenzied celebration as the remaining Croatian players ran onto the field and mobbed their goalkeeper.

And thus, Brazil's hopes for the elusive Hexa would have to wait until at least 2026.

Even in the wake of another soul-crushing early exit from the World Cup, the Brazilian people have every reason to remain optimistic about their beloved national team's future. While the status of the legendary Neymar Jr. for the 2026 World Cup remains uncertain, what is indeed certain is that Brazil has an embarrassment of riches in the form of young, talented, and fundamentally sound players waiting to don the canary yellow tops in future international competitions. And with every passing day, Vinicius Jr. appears more ready to assume the role of team leader and talisman for the squad, destined to one day take the reins from such legendary Brazilian stalwarts as Thiago Silva and the incomparable Neymar Jr.

Chapter 4: Personal Life

Given that the image of Vinicius Jr. can be seen everywhere, from his ubiquitous social media presence to print ads featuring luxury watches to television commercials representing soft drink companies, one might get the idea that the life of the football superstar is an open book. But while it is certain that Vinicius understands how to market himself in today's virtual landscape, when it comes to his personal life, he is more circumspect about how much he reveals to the outside world.

Nowhere is this more apparent than in Vinicius' romantic involvements. Still an unmarried bachelor at 23, Vinicius has been linked with several young women over his time in the public eye. Many observers since 2019 have noted that Vinicius has frequently been spotted with Brazilian model, actress, and influencer Maria Julia Mazalli.[xxxix] Still other more recent accounts have linked him with Kenia Os, a popular Mexican singer.[xl] However, there are signs that Vinicius' is becoming more open about his romantic life, as an increasing number of social media posts have lent credence to the rumored linkage with the Mexican performer.

What is more certain is that Vinicius continues to maintain close relationships with his family and friends, which have served as an important support system for the young star. Vinicius' mother and youngest brother currently live with him in his Madrid home. Also present at the home is a 10-person live-in staff that includes his agent and communications director.[iv]

Additionally, Vinicius retains many of the tight bonds that he developed during his childhood, such as his aunt and uncle, with whom he lived during his academy days at Flamengo. Vini also continues to count the director of the academy at Flemengo, Carlos Noval, as his close friend and mentor, often going to him for advice.[iv]

The fact that Vinicius has achieved worldwide fame yet continues to stay rooted in the world that he grew up in and connected with the people who have helped him along the way is illustrative of what makes him so special. Inside the toned, muscular body of one of soccer's brightest young stars still lives the excitable, smiling, and energetic young boy that he has always been.

According to Gilmar Popoca, one of Vinicius' coaches during his time at Flamengo, the fame that Vini now enjoys has not impacted him in the way that it does so many young athletes. "From my point of view," noted Popoca, "he hasn't changed too much. Of course, the money made a difference to his family, but he is still down to earth. He invites me and my family to his birthday party every year. He treats me with great warmth and respect. He has good people around him."[iv]

Noval, the person credited for discovering Vini at a young age and who facilitated his rise through the academy stage and into the professional ranks, echoes the view espoused by Popoca. Reaffirming Vini's steadfastness in remaining true to his roots in the face of worldwide fame and a robust banking account, Noval remarked of Vini, "He was always a simple, modest kid. Honestly, he might be one of the best people I have met in my life. I mean the human being, not the footballer. He never has a bad word to say about anyone. He always has a grin on his face, always treats everyone exactly the same, even now that he's famous."[iv]

While exact totals remain confidential, at least one recent account predicted Vinicius' net worth at the beginning of 2024 in the neighborhood of $50 million.[xli] This figure is inclusive of Vini's yearly salary at Real Madrid, his various investments that include real estate, gold, and stock market holdings, and his endorsement deals.

Throughout the years, Vinicius has endorsed a wide range of products from all over the world. These companies have included designer watchmaker Golden Concept, One Football, Bet National, Dolce & Gabbana, Pepsi, EA Sports, and Vivo, just to name a few.[xlii]

Perhaps the most prominent of his endorsement deals is the one he has had the longest. Nike, the industry-leading shoe, clothing, and athletic equipment purveyors, first approached Vini to endorse their products when he was just 13 years old.[xlii] Although there had been some recent friction in the relationship between Nike and Vinicius, prompting speculation that the young star might instead endorse a different shoe company such as Adidas or Puma, Vini recently re-signed a new, lucrative contract with Nike.

Philanthropic Work

As Vinicius has continued to maintain the connections that he developed with the many people who assisted him as a child growing up in poverty, he has also given back to his community in a variety of ways. One of the more prominent of his charitable efforts, the Vini Jr. Institute, began in 2020. The focus of the institute, over which Vinicius presides as its president, is to use the wide popularity of soccer among school-aged children in Brazil and apply it to innovations in learning in Brazilian schools. According to the Institute's website, "The

Vini Jr. Institute recognizes the technical and financial limitations of public schools to innovate, as well as the difficulties many low-income families face in tutoring their school-age children, for lack of either time or training, and will therefore work to close those gaps, directly helping improve basic education in Brazil."[xliii]

One of the primary ways that the Vini Jr. Institute has contributed to improving the intersection between education and technology is the creation of the BASE application, an app that helps teachers integrate academic material into a video game format, thus increasing a child's motivation to engage with academic materials in an entertaining manner.

According to the Institute's executive manager, Victor Oliveria, the app is designed to "use the power of football, its playful character, to inspire the kids to learn." On the app, every student has their own account, answering questions drawing on soccer principles to help explain academic subjects such as math or science. As such, a school year is presented as a "season," with each subject constituting a "match." When a student provides a correct answer or successfully completes a unit of study, an avatar of Vini appears on the screen and celebrates in the fashion of a post-goal celebration. The Institute asserts that approximately 4,500 students and 500 teachers have participated in the project across 10 schools throughout the country.

Another aim of the Vini Jr. Institute is to combat the problem of racism through training and education. As such, the institute has created an anti-racism manual and instructed teachers on its use in a school setting. The nearly 70-page manual offers support for schools to improve inclusiveness and deconstruct the harmful stereotypes of minorities and/or low-income students. In addition to the manual, Vinicius has also embarked on a public awareness campaign highlighting the problem of racism utilizing billboards across Brazil. Accompanying a large black-and-white, close-up photograph of Vinicius' face, phrases such as "Racism, don't pretend you don't see it," and "Reveal the racists" adorn the billboards.[xliv]

For his efforts targeting the public good, Vinicius was honored with the 2023 Socrates Award, which is given yearly to acknowledge outstanding charity work by professional soccer players. In accepting the award, presented to him by Prince Albert II of Monaco, Vinicius described the importance of the Institute and its work to those present at the ceremonies. "I will remain strong in the fight against racism," said the Brazilian. "It is a very sad thing to talk about racism nowadays, but we have to continue in the fight so that people suffer less." Continuing,

Vinicius added that he was, "Very happy to receive this award and to help many children in Brazil. I had little chance of getting where I have coming from where I came so it is a pleasure for me to help as many kids as I can so they can have a chance."[xlv]

Chapter 5: Future and Legacy

The challenges of foretelling the future of such a young athlete aside, it can be helpful to take a look at what aided Vinicius' rapid rise to soccer superstardom should he continue a similar trajectory across his career.

Beginning with what sets Vinicius apart from his contemporaries, Vinicius has made his mark with his outstanding speed, energy, explosiveness, sound technique, and most impressively, his remarkable dribbling ability. While it is undeniable that Vinicius experienced trouble finishing in scoring opportunities when first arriving at Real Madrid, he is now seen as one of the most skillful in that area. A matchup nightmare for most defenders, Vinicius excels in one-on-one situations, demonstrating the ability to swiftly and creatively change direction, maintain composure, and finish with authority.

In a soccer landscape where all-time greats such as Leo Messi and Cristiano Ronaldo are preparing to exit the stage and another generation of stars such as Luka Modric, Neymar Jr., and Robert Lewandowski are still performing at a high level but have moved on to the latter half of their distinguished careers, it is a timely pursuit to discuss who will be the players to assume the mantle of soccer's best performers over the next decade. It is easy to identify young players such as the Norwegian striker Erling Haaland, Jude Bellingham of England and, of course, the incomparable Frenchman Kylian Mbappe as the future of international and club soccer.

Furthermore, there is no shortage of soccer journalists, experienced coaches, current and former players, and long-time observers of the beautiful game that make the case that, if Vinicius isn't already the best player in the game, he certainly belongs in the discussion.

According to legendary Real Madrid coach Carlo Ancelotti, Vinicius is already the "best player in the world."[xlvi] Coming from a manager who has had the opportunity to train the likes of Cristiano Ronaldo, Karim Benzema, as well as Vinicius' young teammate Jude Bellingham, this is high praise indeed. Vini's countryman and childhood idol, Neymar Jr., is also on record as to how he feels the young Brazilian stacks up against the other current stars of the game. Following Real Madrid's UEFA Champions League triumph in 2022, Neymar offered, "Mbappe had a great season, Benzema too. But from what I've seen, Vinicius Jr. is the best player in the world."[xlvii]

Meanwhile, former England striker Michael Owen has contended that, not only is Vinicius the most talented player currently, but he's also the most "destructive." Explaining this distinction, Owen explains, "There's not that many people you would say would strike fear into players. When you're going to bed before a game, you're thinking, 'Oh no, I've got to mark him tomorrow', there's not many players.'"[xlviii]

Perhaps more important than metrics, statistics, and the subjective "eye test" is in the effort to determine Vinicius' place in the game relative to his peers, a fuller assessment takes into account both his on-field and off-field contributions. Toward this end, journalist Mark Doyle contends that not only is Vinicius one of today's most talented soccer players but he is also the game's most important player, using his platform as a celebrity athlete to advocate for social change.

Doyle notes that, despite the level of hostility and hatred that he has faced as of late, Vinicius continues to perform at a world-class level, day in and day out. Says Doyle, "The quality of his performances would be praiseworthy in normal circumstances, but they cannot be considered as anything but extraordinary in the climate of toxicity in which he is forced to operate."[xlix]

Arguing that it is unfair that Vinicius is forced to take on this level of responsibility, combatting the scourges of modern life, when by rights he should be having fun playing the game that he loves, Doyle asserts that Vinicius' importance to the game cannot be understated.

If he is worn down by having to bear the burden of being an anti-racism activist in addition to being one of the best soccer players in the world, Vinicius shows no signs of it. Vinicius continues to perform at the highest level on the pitch, and the joyous goal celebrations are still replete with the same samba-dancing abandon that have always been his trademark.

In fact, assuming the mantle of a civil rights icon may have even made him more courageous, both on and off the pitch. Speaking to the French publication *L'equipe*, Vinicius elaborated on how he sees his role in the ongoing battle against racism.

"I know that I, personally, am not going to change history, that I am not going to make Spain a country without racists, nor the whole world, but I know that I can change some things. So that those who come in the next few years do not go through this, so that children can have peace of mind in the future. For them, I will do everything I can."[1]

For his courageous philanthropic and humanitarian efforts, Vinicius was recognized as a Goodwill Ambassador by the United Nations Educational, Scientific, and Cultural Organization (UNESCO) in February 2024. In the press release announcing his selection, UNESCO noted that the "fight for inclusion and against discrimination is particularly important to Vinicius Jr., who has been confronted on numerous occasions with prejudice and racism, in particular from fans. He has worked with FIFA and Brazil to break the silence and promote the values of respect and dialogue, as demonstrated by his participation in the 'Racism, don't pretend you don't see it' campaign."[li]

Vinicius has also been instrumental in influencing the creation and implementation of protocols for soccer leagues to immediately enact and enforce in-game anti-racism measures. Designed to protect players from experiencing the kind of abuse that Vinicius has experienced while sanctioning offending individuals and organizations that do not take decisive action, these efforts have spread from Spain's La Liga to soccer leagues around the world.

Due to his accomplishments on and off the soccer pitch, it is easy to lose sight that Vinicius remains a young athlete, just 23 years of age at the time of this writing. It seems like a forgone conclusion that many more international and club trophies as well as individual accolades lie in his future.

Already included in any list of the best players currently in the game, his youth and considerable experience, when combined with his exuberant and expressive style of play, foretell a long and successful career ahead for Vinicius. To those in Brazil who have known him the best and the longest and witnessed his ascent into stardom, they almost inevitably remark that Vini continues to remain unchanged by the success and fame that he has achieved. He remains the same smiling, joyous, unflappable person that he has always been.

To young Brazilians playing soccer in the streets, who are just becoming aware of him and the space that he occupies in the game today, the name Vinicius now takes on an added dimension. To be certain, they idolize him for his exploits on the pitch and the marvelous things that he can do with a soccer ball at his feet, but these days he means more to them than the sum total of his goal-scoring and other accomplishments. In addition to being a sports hero, he is now admired as a trailblazer and a fighter for equality.

Tracing Vinicius' roots as a young player in Brazil, a journalist recently interviewed several young players at the Flamengo

Academy about what Vinicius means to them today. One player remarked that given the negative attention that Vini has received in European stadiums, the way that he has responded has made him an example for all young black Brazilians to emulate. When asked by the journalist to describe what Vinicius means to him in one word, the unidentified youth responded with the word, "*Superacao*," the Portuguese word for overcoming.[iv]

It's hard to imagine a term more befitting for the emerging athletic superstar turned civil rights activists. The young boy who first overcame long odds to emerge from an impoverished background on the streets of Brazil is now recognized as one of the best young players in the game. Today, in addition to overcoming challenges on the pitch, he is inspiring athletes and non-athletes alike to overcome the obstacles that they face in their own lives.

From economic barriers to learning to the fight for racial equality, Vinicius now stands as an example of how to overcome challenges with tenacity, courage, and determination. More than that, however, Vinicius utilizes the very things that his detractors use against him—his smiling, his dancing, his expressive, exuberant attitude—to blunt the impact of hateful, racist ideology.

As journalist Mark Doyle has asserted, how young black athletes play the game of soccer, from the way they act to how they style their hair, has always met with recriminations on European pitches.[lii] That the phenomenon is not a new one, that it has been an issue for years, is certainly discouraging.

Commenting on the criticism that he has encountered for his exuberant celebrations and flamboyant playing style, Vinicius provided context for his demeanor on the pitch. "Weeks ago, some people started to criticize my dancing. But the dancing is not mine alone," Vinicius said. "They belong to Ronaldinho, Neymar, [Lucas] Paqueta, [Antoine] Griezmann, Joao Felix, Matheus Cunha ... Brazilian funk singers and samba dancers, Latin reggaeton singers, Black Americans. They are dances to celebrate the cultural diversity of the world. They say that happiness bothers. The happiness of a black Brazilian being successful in Europe bothers much more. But my will to win, my smile and the sparkle in my eyes are much bigger than that."[liii]

Despite the discouragement engendered by the blight of the hateful and racist actions of some, the words of support and encouragement that Vinicius has received from so many others is real, growing, and transformative.

No less of an icon than the great Brazilian soccer star Pele, the biggest name in the history of the sport, broadcasted his admiration and support for Vini Jr. In a social media message, Pele reinforced his countryman's position on the current state of affairs in European soccer. "Football is a joy. It's a dance. It's more than that. It's a real party," said the legendary former player whose words perhaps carry the most weight in the worldwide soccer community. Continuing, he asserted, "Although, unfortunately, racism still exists, we will not allow that to stop us from continuing to smile. And we will continue to fight racism every day in this way: fighting for our right to be happy and respected."[liv]

Following in the footsteps of his country's soccer greats and carrying forward the Brazilian spirit in his style of play has already made Vinicius Jr. one of the most interesting and successful young players in the world's most popular game. Vinicius' decision to devote so much of his time, energy, and financial resources toward making the world a better place is transforming him into something grander.

Today, Vinicius is a role model and hero to those who have been impacted by hate and bigotry throughout the world. His determination to stay true to his principles in the face of intense pressure is truly inspirational. While journalists and fans will undoubtedly continue to compare the statistics and performances of players in the ongoing effort to determine who is the best in the game today, it is becoming more and more clear which player has the greatest impact on the game both on and off the pitch. That player is Vinicius Jr., the one who overcomes.

Final Word/About the Author

Wow! You made it to the end of this book, and you're reading the About the Author section? Now that's impressive and puts you in the top 1% of readers.

Since you're curious about me, I was born and raised in Norwalk, Connecticut. Growing up, I could often be found spending many nights watching basketball, soccer, and football matches with my father in the family living room. I love sports and everything that sports can embody. I believe that sports are one of the most genuine forms of competition, heart, and determination. I write my works to learn more about influential athletes in the hopes that from my writing, you the reader can walk away inspired to put in an equal if not greater amount of hard work and perseverance to pursue your goals.

I've written these stories for over a decade, and loved every moment of it. When I look back on my life, I am most proud of not just having covered so many different athletes' inspirational stories, but for all the times I got e-mails or handwritten letters from readers on the impact my books have had on them.

So thank you from the bottom of my heart for allowing me to do work I find meaningful. I am incredibly grateful for you and your support.

If you're new to my sports biography books, welcome. I have goodies for you as a thank you from me in the pages ahead.

Before we get there though, I have a question for you...

Were you inspired at any point in this book?
If so, would you help someone else get inspired too?

You see, my mission is to inspire sports fans of all ages around the world that anything is possible through hard work and perseverance...but the only way to accomplish this mission is by reaching everyone.

So here's my ask from you:

Most people, regardless of what the saying tells them to do, judge a book by its cover (and its reviews).

If you enjoyed *Vinicius Junior: The Inspiring Story of One of Soccer's Star Forwards,* please help inspire another person needing to hear this story by leaving a review.

Doing so takes less than a minute, and that dose of inspiration can change another person's life in more ways than you can even imagine.

To get that generous 'feel good' feeling and help another person, all you have to do is take 60 seconds and leave a review.

☆☆☆☆☆ ✍

<u>If you're on Audible</u>: hit the three dots in the top right of your device, click rate & review, then leave a few sentences about the book with a star rating.

<u>If you're reading on Kindle or an e-reader</u>: scroll to the bottom of the book, then swipe up and it will prompt a review for you.

<u>If for some reason these have changed</u>: you can head back to Amazon and leave a review right on the book's page.

Thank you for helping another person, and for your support of my writing as an independent author.

Clayton

Like what you read?
Then you'll love these too!

This book is one of hundreds of stories I've written. If you enjoyed this story on Vinicius Junior, you'll love my other sports biography book series too.

You can find them by visiting my website at claytongeoffreys.com or by scanning the QR code below to follow my author page on Amazon.

Soccer Biography Books: This series covers the stories of tennis greats such as Neymar, Harry Kane, Robert Lewandowski, and more.

Basketball Biography Books: This series covers the stories of over 100 NBA greats such as Stephen Curry, LeBron James, Michael Jordan, and more.

Football Biography Books: This series covers the stories of over 50 NFL greats such as Peyton Manning, Tom Brady, and Patrick Mahomes, and more.

Baseball Biography Books: This series covers the stories of over 40 MLB greats such as Aaron Judge, Shohei Ohtani, Mike Trout, and more.

Basketball Leadership Biography Books: This series covers the stories of basketball coaching greats such as Steve Kerr, Gregg Popovich, John Wooden, and more.

Tennis Biography Books: This series covers the stories of tennis greats such as Serena Williams, Rafael Nadal, Andy Roddick, and more.

Women's Basketball Biography Books: This series covers the stories of many WNBA greats such as Diana Taurasi, Sue Bird, Sabrina Ionescu, and more.

Lastly, if you'd like to join my exclusive list where I let you know about my latest books, and gift you free copies of some of my other books, go to **claytongeoffreys.com/goodies**.

Or, if you don't like typing, scan the following QR code here to go there directly. See you there!

[QR code: SCAN ME]

Clayton

References

[i] Bonn, Kyle. "Vinicius Jr Contract, Salary at Real Madrid: Brazil Star Signs New Deal with Los Blancos through 2027." *Sporting News*, 31 Oct. 2023. Web.
[ii] Strans, Susan. "Vini Jr Net Worth 2024." *Equity Atlas*, 1 Dec. 2023. Web.
[iii] Hendrix, Hale. "Vinicius Junior Childhood Story Plus Untold Biography Facts." *LifeBlogger*, 3 Jan. 2024. Web.
[iv] Lang, Jack. "In Search of Vinicius Junior - the 22-Year-Old 'Raising a Flag for Everyone.'" *The Athletic*, 28 May 2022, theathletic.com. Web.
[v] Lang, Dermot Corrigan and Jack. "The Rise of Vinicius Junior and How Ancelotti Brought His Real Career to Life." *The Athletic*, 28 May 2022, theathletic.com. Web.
[vi] OneFootball. "Real Madrid Attacker Vinicius Junior: Futsal and Street Football Helped Me." *OneFootball*, 26 Apr. 2021, onefootball.com. Web.
[vii] Panja, Tariq. "Old Friends and Family Recipes Fuel a Real Madrid Prodigy." *The New York Times*, The New York Times, 26 July 2019, www.nytimes.com. Web.
[viii] "Flamengo Call up Vinicius to First Team Training." *MARCA*, 9 May 2017, www.marca.com. Web.
[ix] As.com. "Vinicius Junior: Flamengo Starlet Makes Professional Debut." *Diario AS*, 14 May 2017. Web.
[x] Jhaveri, Parth. "Barcelona's Former Scout Reveals Vinicius Junior Betrayal." *Everything Barca*, Everything Barca, 14 Apr. 2021, Web.
[xi] Janeiro, Virtudes Sanchez de. "Vinicius: Real Madrid or Barcelona? I Want to Play for the Biggest Club in the World." *MARCA in English*, 13 June 2017. Web.
[xii] *FIFA's Regulations on the Status and Transfer of Players*, www.icsspe.org/system/files/FIFA - Regulations on the Status and Transfer of Players.pdf. Web.
[xiii] Simpson, Christopher. "Vinicius Jr. Will Reportedly Leave Flamengo, Join Real Madrid for Pre-Season." *Bleacher Report*, Bleacher Report, 25 June 2018, bleacherreport.com. Web.
[xiv] MailOnline, James Dutton. "Vinicius Junior Tears up during His Final Press Conference for Flamengo before Joining Real Madrid." *Daily Mail Online*, Associated Newspapers, 26 June 2018, www.dailymail.co.uk. Web.
[xv] "Video: Vinicius Jr's Flamengo Career." *BeSoccer Livescore: All Today's Live Soccer Scores*, 13 May 2022, www.besoccer.com. Web.
[xvi] Villacreses, Jose. "Quotes from Vinicius' Press Conference with Real Madrid." *Managing Madrid*, Managing Madrid, 20 July 2018,

www.managingmadrid.com. Web.

[xvii] Velayudhan, Adithya. "Twitter Erupts as Vinicius Jr Impresses on Real Madrid Debut versus Manchester United." *Sportskeeda*, Sportskeeda, 5 Aug. 2018, www.sportskeeda.com. Web.

[xviii] Sharpe, Sam. "Match Report: Atlético Madrid B 2-2 Real Madrid Castilla." *Managing Madrid*, Managing Madrid, 3 Sept. 2018, www.managingmadrid.com. Web.

[xix] McCormack, Kristofer. "The Matches That Made Vinicius Junior." *Managing Madrid*, 10 June 2022, www.managingmadrid.com. Web.

[xx] "Vinicius: I'll Never Forget Real Madrid Debut." *FotMob*, FotMob, 30 Sept. 2018, www.fotmob.com. Web.

[xxi] "Alavés 1-0 Real Madrid (Oct 6, 2018) Game Analysis." *ESPN*, ESPN Internet Ventures, 6 Oct. 2018, www.espn.com. Web.

[xxii] Marsden, Sam. "Coronavirus Crisis: La Liga Suspended Indefinitely." *ESPN*, ESPN Internet Ventures, 23 Mar. 2020, www.espn.com. Web.

[xxiii] Martín, Agustín. "Real Madrid: Meet Vinicius Junior's Personal Fitness Trainer Thiago Lobo." *Diario AS*, 26 Mar. 2020, en.as.com. Web.

[xxiv] "La Liga to Resume on 11 June; 2020-21 Season to Start in September." *BBC Sport*, BBC, 29 May 2020, www.bbc.com. Web.

[xxv] "Real Madrid 1-0 Real Valladolid (30 Sep, 2020) Game Analysis - ESPN (UK)." *ESPN*, 30 Sept. 2020, www.espn.co.uk. Web.

[xxvi] "Levante 0-2 Real Madrid: Vinicius Junior and Karim Benzema Score." *BBC Sport*, BBC, 4 Oct. 2020, www.bbc.com. Web.

[xxvii] MacEvoy, Sam. "Real Madrid: Tunnel Footage Reveals Karim Benzema Laying into Team-Mate Vinicius at Half-Time." *Daily Mail Online*, Associated Newspapers, 29 Oct. 2020, www.dailymail.co.uk. Web.

[xxviii] Carpio, Carlos, and Adapted by SAM. "Benzema Does Pass to Vinicius." *MARCA*, Marca, 13 May 2022, www.marca.com. Web.

[xxix] "Real Madrid 3-1 Liverpool (Apr 6, 2021) Game Analysis." *ESPN*, ESPN Internet Ventures, 6 Apr. 2021, www.espn.com. Web.

[xxx] R, Pranav. "The Rise of Vinicius Jr: From an Underwhelming Starlet to a Bernabeu Cult Icon." *Medium*, Medium, 2 Dec. 2022, medium.com. Web.

[xxxi] Navarrete, Lucas. "Levante vs Real Madrid, 2021 La Liga: Immediate Reaction." *Managing Madrid*, Managing Madrid, 22 Aug. 2021, www.managingmadrid.com. Web.

[xxxii] Salvi, Sudhir. "Real Madrid: 3 Ways in Which Vinicius Junior Has Improved This Season." *The Real Champs*, The Real Champs, 4 Nov. 2021, therealchamps.com. Web.

[xxxiii] Kirkland, Alex. "Vinicius Junior Abuse Timeline: What Happened next for Real Madrid, LaLiga, More." *ESPN*, ESPN Internet Ventures, 2 June

2023, www.espn.com. Web.

[xxxiv] Jr., Vini. "Não Foi a Primeira Vez, Nem a Segunda e Nem a Terceira. O Racismo É o Normal Na La Liga. A Competição Acha Normal, a Federação Também e Os Adversários Incentivam. Lamento Muito. O Campeonato Que Já Foi de Ronaldinho, Ronaldo, Cristiano e Messi Hoje É Dos Racistas. Uma Nação..." *Twitter*, Twitter, 21 May 2023, twitter.com. Web.

[xxxv] Corrigan, Dermot. "Vinicius Junior and Racism in Spanish Football - Has Anything Changed?" *The Athletic*, 24 Oct. 2023, theathletic.com. Web.

[xxxvi] Daz, Jos Flix. "Brazil Push to Have Vinicius at the Copa America." *MARCA in English*, 23 Apr. 2019, www.marca.com. Web.

[xxxvii] Piacenti, Jennifer. "2022 World Cup Odds - Sports Illustrated." *2022 World Cup Odds*, 16 Nov. 2022, www.si.com. Web.

[xxxviii] Ferreira, Luana. "Brazilians Want One Thing from Their Football Team: Hexa." *Al Jazeera*, Al Jazeera, 9 Dec. 2022, www.aljazeera.com. Web.

[xxxix] Micallef, Catherine. "Get to Know Brazil Winger Vinicius Jr Girlfriend Maria Julia Mazalli." *The US Sun*, The US Sun, 13 Sept. 2023, www.the-sun.com. Web.

[xl] Smm. "Vinicius Confirms Romance with Kenia OS: Who Is the Mexican Woman the Soccer Player Has Fallen in Love With?" *MARCA*, Marca, 18 July 2023, www.marca.com. Web.

[xli] "Vinicius Junior's Net Worth in 2024 [Detailed and Updated]." *SureBets*, 1 Feb. 2024, surebets.bet. Web.

[xlii] Garcia-Ochoa, Juan Ignacio. "The 'Vini Jr' Empire." *MARCA*, Marca, 3 Feb. 2023, www.marca.com. Web.

[xliii] "Home - Instituto Vini Jr." *Instituto Vini Jr*, 9 May 2023, institutovinijr.org. Web.

[xliv] Garcia, Adriana. "Vinícius Júnior Launches Campaign to Combat Racism in Brazil." *ESPN*, ESPN Internet Ventures, www.espn.com. Web.

[xlv] *Vinicius Vows to Continue Fight against Racism as He Wins Socrates ...*, 30 Oct. 2023, www.reuters.com. Web.

[xlvi] Rai, Guillermo, and Colin Millar. "Vinicius Jr 'best in the World' - Ancelotti." *The Athletic*, The Athletic, 10 Feb. 2024, theathletic.com. Web.

[xlvii] Booth, Chuck. "Neymar Calls Vinicius Jr. the World's Best Player Ahead of Karim Benzema and Kylian Mbappe." *CBSSports.Com*, 29 May 2022, www.cbssports.com. Web.

[xlviii] Lewis, Mason. "Real Madrid's Vinicius Junior the 'most Destructive Player' in World Football, Says Michael Owen." *Eurosport*, Eurosport, 17 May 2023, www.eurosport.com. Web.

[xlix] Doyle, Mark. "Vinicius Jr: The Most Important Player in Football."

Goal.Com US, Goal.com, 21 Mar. 2024, www.goal.com. Web.

[l] Bourlon, Antoine. "Vinicius Jr.: ' Si Je Suis Seul Face Au Racisme, Le Système va m'écraser .'" *L'Équipe*, L'Équipe, 2 Jan. 2024, www.lequipe.fr. Web.

[li] UNESCO. "Vinícius Junior Named UNESCO Goodwill Ambassador." *UNESCO.Org*, 2 Feb. 2024, www.unesco.org. Web.

[lii] Doyle, Mark. "Vinicius Jr: The Ultimate Role Model Who Must Never Stop Dancing." *Goal.Com US*, Goal.com, 19 Sept. 2023, www.goal.com, Web.

[liii] "Real's Vinicius Jr Hits Back at 'racist' Celebration Critic." *BBC Sport*, BBC, 17 Sept. 2022, www.bbc.com/sport/football/62938446. Web.

[liv] Espn FC. "Pele Released a Statement on Vini Jr. and His Dancing. Pic.Twitter.Com. Twitter.com. Web.

Made in the USA
Middletown, DE
05 March 2025